THE LONDON HARNESS HORSE

Parade

A BRIEF HISTORY

THE LONDON HARNESS HORSE

Parade

A BRIEF HISTORY

Keith Chivers

J. A. Allen

First edition 1985

2nd edition published 1996

ISBN 0–85131–690–5

Published in Great Britain by
J. A. Allen & Company Limited
1 Lower Grosvenor Place, Buckingham Palace Road
London SW1W 0EL

Book production Bill Ireson

Printed in Hong Kong

TO ALL THOSE

who over a period of a hundred years have freely given
their time, energy and knowledge to the London Cart
and Van Horse Parades and the London Harness
Horse Parade as organisers, judges, veterinary inspectors, stewards, commentators, catalogue-distributors
and in other ways; to all participants – owners, drivers,
assistants and passengers; to those who have been
responsible for the preservation and beauty of the
Regent's Park and have been the Parades' kindly
hosts; to the officials and members of the R.S.P.C.A.
and of those breed societies and other organisations
which have given practical support; to the Home of
Rest for Horses, which supplies its horse ambulance;
to all subscribers and sponsors; to the Metropolitan
Police, who have ensured the safety of Londoners
peacefully assembling to watch; to the St. John's
Ambulance Brigade; to the spectators, without whom
the Parades would have been no fun and would have
perished long ago; to everyone who has helped to
maintain not only the very serious purpose for which
the constituent Societies were founded but also their
amiable spirit and especially the many whose names
do not appear in this brief story but who, in a longer
and more leisurely-told version, would have been
mentioned by name for their exceptional service over a
long period of time; and, in particular, to the memory
of the first Sir Walter Gilbey and of the Baroness
Burdett-Coutts who started the London Cart Horse
Parade in 1885

THIS BOOK IS DEDICATED

Contents

Acknowledgements

This book owes much to the generous help of Coutts and Company, Bankers to the Society since 1887. And I extend my thanks to the present Committee of the London Harness Horse Parade, who asked me to write it and allowed me to carry out so enjoyable a task in my own way. I am particularly grateful to Walter Gilbey and John Young for strongly encouraging and supporting me and for their detailed and constructive comments. To Harry Gates I am also obliged for his helpful corrections.

For the first 30 years of the Cart Horse Parade, I owe much to the late R. A. Brown, who allowed me in 1969 to make copious notes from documents then in his possession, but which have since disappeared. Most of the constituent Societies' other records had already been lost, and any coherent account would have been virtually impossible had not the *Times* been in the habit for many years of reporting Parades at considerable length.

Bernard B. Murdock, whose expert knowledge of London tradesmen's horses and vehicles is founded on practical experience, has been typically generous in allowing me to make use of his fine collection of photographs, precisely documented. I am indebted for their interest and help also to Bridget Williams, Sainsbury's Company Archivist; T. W. Baker-Jones, Archivist of W. H. Smith and Son Limited; F. R. Clark, Museum Curator, North Thames Gas; L. C. Marsh of Charringtons Solid Fuel Limited; Len Overall; and Victor Yates, Company Archivist and Historian of Selfridges.

The Local History Librarian of Wandsworth Borough Council and the Local Studies Librarian of the Royal Borough of Kensington and Chelsea went out of their way to rescue me from ignorance and uncertainty.

My further thanks are due to Sylvia Newton who, in typing the manuscript, managed to follow the intended route and to remove confusing signposts still remaining after the abandonment, in the cause of brevity, of many curious diversions.

I wish to record my thanks to the following for supplying illustrations or for allowing pictures in their ownership to be used:

(Page numbers in parentheses)

Illustrated London News Picture Library (28–29; 39; 41, bottom; 42; 50; 53 and 54)
BBC Hulton Picture Library (22; 34–35; 36 and 38)
Bernard B. Murdock (51; 55; 56; 57; 68; 69 and 70)
Amenities Committee of the London Borough of Tower Hamlets (15)
Walter A. Gilbey (17)
Wandsworth Public Libraries (24–25)
Charringtons Solid Fuel Limited (43)
Mrs. J. Bryant (41, top)
Selfridges Archives (63)
J. Sainsbury plc (66)
W. H. Smith and Son Limited (67)
Times Newspapers Limited (74)
Unigate Dairies Limited (76)
John A. Young (77 and cover)
Michael Franklin (78)
Lingwood Shire Promotions (84)
L.H.H.P. Society (87)

1 Friends of the Cart Horse 1885

A London parade of horses and vehicles in spring-time was not, in 1885, an entirely new idea. In the old time before the railways, all the mail coaches were assembled every May Day at Millbank where their proprietors, after a mid-day banquet provided by the contractor for His Majesty's mails, were able to watch them being inspected. And a glorious sight they were to see – new coaches making their first appearance, old ones newly painted and furnished; coachmen and guards in new liveries of scarlet and gold; horses look-ing their finest. The judges were hard put to it in choosing the winners.

Then the procession made its way, between dense and cheering crowds, through the Strand, Fleet Street and Ludgate Hill to the General Post Office – Lombard Street until 1829 and thereafter St. Martin's-le-Grand. On this special occasion every seat, as the coaches left for all parts of England, was usually taken.

The railways, which finished off the flying mail-coach horse, played his heavyweight walking brother a quite different trick. By enabling industry and com-merce to expand at a fantastic rate, they immensely increased his labours. Most of the freight hauled by steam began its journey behind a plodding horse and had to complete it behind another.

At Liverpool in the 1850s people began to celebrate May Day by showing off their cart horses in various parts of the city and, in an attempt to recapture some of the old country spirit, decked them fantastically with flowers. In 1863 these unorganised and scattered jol-lifications were consolidated into one great civic event. The Liverpool May Day Parade became famous, and was the fun-loving father of the London Cart Horse Parade.

As for its reforming mother, her pedigree can be

11

traced back to the foundation in 1826, amid much scoffing, of the Society for the Prevention of Cruelty to Animals. For many years its supporters bore a heavy load on a slow and uphill route, unassisted either by law or by public opinion. The lot of the London dray horse in 1885 was still on the whole a disgrace to civilised society.

The foul air and hard pavements, detrimental to his lungs and legs, made excellent management a necessity. Some horses received it, but more did not. Many were grossly over-worked. Their collars were not uncommonly too small, and choked them; or too big, and rubbed them sore; or had filthy and lumpy linings. Harness was frequently defective, or improperly adjusted, or the angle of draught was incorrect. Feet were first neglected and then excessively pared and rasped to make them fit a shoe. Injuries and sores went untreated. Stables were too often draughty, or damp, or unventilated, or dirty. Grooming was sometimes utterly neglected. The horse has a delicate digestive system, but feeding and watering were in many cases bad or thoughtless. Parasites, external and internal, were left to flourish. Regulations about contagious diseases such as glanders (then, not surprisingly, rampant) were either ignored or deliberately frustrated.

Those employers who treated their men as human beings were almost always those who also looked properly after their horses. The others, who were legion, were especially foolish because in monetary terms the horse was more valuable than the man he worked with. If a man became worn out or useless, they hired another. To replace a horse, they had to buy one.

Positive cruelty by employees also played its part, and public opinion was as uneducated about this as it had been earlier about little children in mines, chimneys or factories. Just two people had so far made any impression upon the Londoner's conscience in this matter. Anna Sewell, an elderly semi-invalid spinster living in Brighton, had caused something of a sensation with her book *Black Beauty*, published in 1877. Her account of the good Mr. Wright, who took vigorous action when he saw a drunken carter knocking his horses about, makes it clear that he was a man in a hundred. Miss Sewell never wrote another book, and was now dead. But the other influential campaigner against cruelty to animals, the Baroness Burdett-Coutts, was very much alive.

By the 1880s, the Liverpool Parade was no longer a mere spree. Thanks to Richard Reynolds, the Corporation's Veterinary Surgeon, horses were examined and rosettes awarded to those which showed clear signs of regular good treatment. The Manchester May Day Parade, its first imitator, had adopted similar arrangements. Now a third society, in Bristol, had been founded expressly for this humanitarian purpose, and a visit to its second Parade, in 1885, will be instructive.

The introduction of Bank Holidays fourteen years earlier had made Whit Monday an obvious choice of date, and 749 horses assembled that morning in the Cattle Market. (It was to take London eleven years to beat this number and, by then, the Bristol society had collapsed. The congenital cause of its early death may be diagnosed by some readers, even from a brief look at the arrangements.) Twelve judges examined the horses and their harness, watched by those members of the public prepared to pay half-a-crown to get in. This took two hours. Then the drivers and their charges emerged, to enthusiastic cheering never accorded them on other days of the year. They paraded through the city and up to Clifton, round the outside of the Zoo and back to the Victoria Rooms – 5½ miles. On such a hilly route, vehicles were impracticable because slow ones would hold up the faster. So the horses, though in harness, were led, and wore a placard round the neck, proclaiming whose they were. People could not make out the writing except by darting, to their imminent danger, into the road. So it was decided that next time two placards should be worn, one on each side. The whole way was lined with spectators – tightly packed and tumultuous in the town, but sparser on the genteel pavements of Clifton. No one could remember such vast crowds.

13

OPPOSITE
*Some owners could –
and did – buy good
horses, well up to the
work required of
them, and looked after
them properly.
Among these were the
Metropolitan Board of
Works and the
Vestries, using public
money. This dust cart
is in Old Montague
Street, E1*

The following Saturday 700 persons – drivers, city fathers and guests – sat down to a substantial meal in the Colston Hall. At the end of it, those men who had been commended for the condition of their horses and harness queued to receive a ten shilling prize and certificate. Then the others lined up and were given half-a-crown. The boredom of these proceedings was alleviated by the City of Bristol Police Band, whose powerful efforts stimulated, but effectively drowned, sporadic shouts and cheers from the jolly diners.

Funds were ample. Civic pride had been whipped up by the combined efforts of the City Council, the Master of the Merchant Venturers and other leading citizens such as Colonel Savile the organiser and J. C. Wall, who horsed a large part of the Great Western Railway. Even before the first Parade had taken place the year before, the public had subscribed, in small amounts, the sum of £300, equivalent to about £9,000 at our centenary values.

Two of the seven speeches at the dinner evoked specially loud cheers. The High Sheriff said he had received intelligence that very afternoon which suggested that peace was now assured: Britain and Russia would remain friends. The Lord Mayor's great moment came when he announced that his advice had been sought by "the London people", who wanted to have their own Parade. Bristolians could never forget that theirs had once been the second city in the Kingdom.

Who were these London people? Who was in a position there to organise a Parade? Bristol, Manchester and Liverpool, like other provincial towns, had enjoyed semi-democratic local government for exactly fifty long years – ever since the Municipal Reform Act had given ratepayers the right to vote in council elections. Only Londoners had been forgotten, as usual. They had no elected governing body. Like the folk of Hinton-in-the-Hedges or Hogsthorpe, or Uplyme or Down Hatherley, they still lived in "parishes" surrounding the ancient City and had only their Vestries. For just thirty years, it is true, over-all management of some matters had been entrusted to the Metropolitan

14

15

OPPOSITE
*Walter Gilbey, sixth
son of a Bishop's
Stortford coach
proprietor, was born
in 1831. He and his
brother Alfred, with
barely a sovereign
between them, set up
in the wine trade after
returning from the
Crimean War*

Board of Works, set up by an Act of 1855. Starting as a sanitary authority, it had done other good things – introducing building regulations, constructing some new streets, abolishing tolls on the Thames bridges. But it could not become a focus of civic pride. It was unsatisfactory even as a target of civic discontent, for the people did not elect it. Its members were nominated by the thirty-nine Vestry Boards, and if a nominee proved useless, it was reckoned to require at least twelve years before he could be removed. The Metropolitan Board of Works had no power, even if it had the wish, to start a Cart Horse Parade.

The initiator was Walter Gilbey. And who more appropriate? Everyone knew him. He and his brother had brought value-for-money wine to the people of Britain – cheap and sold in the grocers' shops. Of every fourteen men in the whole of the United Kingdom who bought a bottle of wine, and of every thirty-nine that bought a bottle of spirits, one of each was a customer of W. & A. Gilbey, the biggest business of its kind in the world. Tall, thin and monocled, Walter was a popular figure.

He had long been devoted to the improvement of horses, and was a founder-member of the English Cart Horse Society in 1878. In its very first year, he proposed that, to give the breed a clear and distinctive name like its rivals the Suffolk and Clydesdale, it should be called the "Shire" instead. The new-fangled title was adopted in 1884, the year when he was President.

This Shire Horse Society, under the patronage of the Prince of Wales, was already both powerful and prestigious. Mr. Gilbey suggested that it might organise a London Cart Horse Parade. The Council decided that it could not meddle in local matters, even if the locality was London. And its duty was to promote one breed: although the Shire was the heavy haulier *par excellence*, London horses were of various breeds and types, including Continental ones. However, the Duke of Westminster, Mr. Gilbey's successor as President, promised his personal support. So did Colonel the Honourable Edward Coke (third President, and

16

17

younger son of "Coke of Norfolk", 1st Earl of Leicester) and many others.

Mr. Gilbey then approached Baroness Burdett-Coutts, whom he had already persuaded to cough up a guinea to join the Shire Horse Society. Long ago, only two months after Queen Victoria came to the throne in 1837, when she was Angela Burdett and twenty-three years old, she had inherited the fortune of her grandfather, the banker Thomas Coutts. This was reputed to be £1,800,000, the equivalent of nearly £40,000,000 today. She became Miss Coutts, the friend of Wellington and Dickens, doer of good deeds whose number and variety, from helping prostitutes to promoting education, was staggering. It was not just her money that made her the most popular person in London among ordinary people, for her donations were mostly anonymous and unfathomable. She was called Queen of the Poor, Queen of the Costermongers. In 1871, the Queen of England had made her a Baroness in her own right, then a unique distinction. The Prince of Wales said that she was, "the most remarkable woman, next to my mother, in the Kingdom".

She had worked hard for the R.S.P.C.A. and, welcoming the Parade idea, promised that her young husband W. Ashmead Bartlett (now called William Burdett-Coutts) should be President. If Mr. Gilbey, who had been thinking of the Duke of Westminster for this, was taken aback, he was too polite to show it. Anyway, Mr. Burdett-Coutts was keen on horses and, since his marriage, could afford to breed them. And he had just become M.P. for Westminster.

A committee was formed, and included the two greatest authorities on equine health and disease, Professors Axe and Pritchard of the Royal Veterinary College; Thomas Brewis, of Brewis Brothers, the Tyne Main Coal Company, King's Cross; Herbert Rymill, proprietor of the Royal City Repository in the Barbican, where many of the best heavy horses were bought and sold; J. H. Raffety, manager of the Agricultural Hall at Islington, venue of the great four-day Shire Horse Show every February; and John Sloughgrove, secretary of the Shire Horse Society. W. H. Mole,

M.R.C.V.S., of the R.S.P.C.A. was appointed Secretary. John Colam, secretary of the R.S.P.C.A., agreed to be Parade Organiser. Robert Ruthven Pym, partner in Coutts' bank, became Honorary Treasurer. Chairman, Walter Gilbey. Patron, H.R.H. Duke of Cambridge. Their declared object was "to improve the general condition and treatment of the London cart horses by encouraging the drivers to take a humane interest in the animals under their charge".

It was now too late to hold a parade this year, even on August Bank Holiday. It was therefore planned to begin on Whit Monday, 1886.

2 Battersea Park to Regent's Park 1886–1889

In London 14th June 1886 was dull and drizzly. But weather did not deter Victorians from making holiday. At Lords, they played all day and the South of England began their reply to the North's 305 in a sort of twilight. They batted until 7 p.m. by which time they were 79 runs for 3 wickets, Dr. W. G. Grace having contributed 32.

Hundreds of excursion trains laid on by the London, Brighton and South Coast and the London, Chatham and Dover companies were crammed, as were those on the London, Tilbury and Southend and the North London lines. The Great Eastern carried 120,000 trippers that day and even the longer-distance specials of the GNR, MR, GWR and LSWR were packed out. For the humble poor, it was possible to combine a day of drinking with any free show that might be going. News about what was happening in Battersea Park had spread and a vast crowd converged upon it.

Early in the morning Mr. Burdett-Coutts and two eminent members of the Shire Horse Society's Council, Anthony Hamond and P. Albert Muntz, M.P., who were to judge the horses, met the stewards in Battersea at the Dogs' Home and Professor Pritchard stationed himself at the entrance to the Park. He was soon examining horses as they entered – ready to turn away those unsuited to the size of the vehicles they were hauling and those which were poor, filthy or diseased. But there were not many of these, because the Parade was open only to animals which had already won a prize at some local event. Since there was no entry fee, this was a wise precaution, because there was no way of guessing how many would take part. No one knew how many heavy horses there were in London, anyway.

Eager spectators hemmed the sweating judges in so tight that they could scarcely do their work. Eventually they accepted all those that the Professor had admitted – eighty single-horse turnouts, twelve pairs, six unicorn teams (two abreast and one in front) and four teams of four. The City Sewers Commission was represented by six singles, and four Vestries (Clerkenwell, St. Marylebone, Islington and St. George's Hanover Square) sent a total of twenty. Among the coal merchants, Brewis Brothers and Tyne Main (both in the same ownership) sent six each, and D. Radford and Company twelve. The Champion Vinegar Company exhibited three singles, two pairs and a unicorn. Fouracre's Brewery entered four teams of matched threes – chestnut, bay, black and grey. Messrs. Pictor, who showed two teams of four drawing flat trucks, had loaded them with stone from their famous Wiltshire quarries – apparently unaware that the general idea was to mark the holiday by carrying drivers' wives, children, aunts, grandmothers, great-uncles and as many other relations and neighbours as could be accommodated without any falling off except the over-adventurous or the already inebriated.

Every driver was awarded a cash prize – ten shillings (50p) for teams, seven-and-six for pairs, and five shillings for singles. The judges were so pleased with some that they gave them a double premium and these also received an R.S.P.C.A. diploma from Mr. Colam in recognition of the evident care they took of their horses throughout the year. The total expenses, £53, were met by Mr. Burdett-Coutts and Mr. Gilbey.

The philippic movement was gathering momentum, and it was in this same year that the Home of Rest for Horses was founded. It did not provide permanent residence for the aged, as a modern reader might assume. It was far more practical, for its objects were to enable the poorer classes to procure rest and skilled treatment for their animals when needed, and in the mean time to provide "temps".

The Graphic artist's eye in 1887 was caught by (top) John Ford and his 23-year-old horse Charles, which he had driven for 17 years and which now won a red rosette. There is no knowing now, unfortunately, who they worked for. One of the three judges is examining a mane (centre). Wellington (below), one of four singles entered by Alex Gordon of the Caledonian Road

Whit Monday in 1887 was as drizzly as the year before, but no one minded much, because all London was working itself into a frenzy for the Queen's Golden Jubilee. The Parade was thrown open to all heavy horses stabled within a seven-mile radius of Charing Cross. If all had come, there would have been about twenty thousand or so, but in the event 383, attached to 278 vehicles, were admitted by Professor Pritchard. There was no intolerable congestion this time, because judging was done in the grounds of the Albert Palace.

Battersea Park had been suggested by the Prince Consort in 1851 as the best permanent site for the Crystal Palace after the Great Exhibition. His proposal was over-ruled but Battersea now at last had a consolation prize. The great glass and iron structure built for the National Exhibition in Dublin had been transported there, and opened in 1885. The principal building, with a gallery all round, was 473 feet long and 84 wide, and had an apse of 50 feet by 84. The double-galleried Connaught Hall, 157 feet by 118, housed the second most powerful organ in Europe, with 67 stops and 4,200 pipes, a carillon of 61 bells and many of the extra boxes of tricks later found in cinema organs. A two-storey brick and stone building, 473 feet long, housed picture galleries, dining saloons, a kitchen where 50,000 meals could be prepared, smoking rooms, reading rooms and shops for the sale of knick-knacks.

Spectators who wanted to watch the judging against this luxurious background were charged a shilling, which provoked much general disapproval, vociferously expressed. However, people without a shilling could stand in the Park and see the competitors arrive and depart. The huge crowd that did so regained its spirits when Lady Burdett-Coutts drove through to present the prizes, and she was given many a hearty cheer.

Mr. Muntz and two more prominent Shire men, T. A. Spencer and C. W. Tindall, selected 119 drivers to receive red rosettes (a new idea) as well as the money prizes, and the majority of the others won a consola-

The Albert Exhibition Palace in Battersea Park. The apse, clearly visible on the left, was centrally placed on the 473-foot frontage of the exhibition hall. The stone and brick building, with picture galleries above and dining saloons, kitchens and other amenities on the ground floor, lay behind to the south, and cannot be seen here. The Connaught Hall, usually called the Annexe, housed the great organ which the Graphic in 1885 claimed to be superior even to the famous one at Haarlem "in the points of magnitude, tone, balance of power and constructive art"

tion blue rosette. There was a small gratuity for drivers who did not earn a cash award – a pleasant gesture, because of course they were not paid for enjoying themselves with their employers' property on a Bank Holiday. R.S.P.C.A. diplomas were awarded to forty-six entrants.

The judges also chose twenty-eight singles, twelve pairs and six teams to proceed across Chelsea Bridge to Olympia, where there was another and quite distinct competition, for the best horses of any recognisable breed. To enable this to be judged, the Bank Holiday pony and donkey races were interrupted. St. Marylebone Vestry won first prize for singles, with St. George's Hanover Square second and third. Holland and Hannen the builders had the best pair and Courage and Company the winning team. There were twelve prizes, all given by the Olympia Company. The Parade itself had been supported by subscriptions from several benevolent persons and, when all expenses were paid, there was a balance at Messrs. Coutts and Co's bank in the Strand of three shillings and seven pence.

Early in 1888, the Albert Palace suddenly closed down. (A few years later, it was demolished and replaced by blocks of mansions.) So by permission of Her Majesty's First Commissioner of Works the Parade was transferred to Regent's Park. It was not permitted to charge spectators, even if a separate judging area could have been secured, and chaos was therefore confidently expected on such a lovely warm day. However, a large contingent of police and an army of stewards kept perfect order and ensured plenty of room for the inspections.

Both Professor Pritchard and the judges applied a more rigorous standard this year, determined to urge forward the objects of the Society. Single-horsed vehicles increased to 222, but a drop in pairs and teams kept the total down to 278, the same as the year before. The main disappointment was that none of the railway companies participated. Brewers were outnumbered by distillers. Coal merchants and Vestries continued to be the best supporters.

The Shire Horse Society now offered prizes similar to those given by the Olympia Company the year before. Its two special judges, working side by side with the Parade judges (who, as usual, were also Shire men, except for L. S. Wilson of the Suffolk Horse Society) cast prejudice behind them and included three Suffolks and a Clydesdale among the twelve winners. Naturally, they ignored those ugly Belgians with their bunched-up heads, and anything else that looked foreign.

After five hours' continuous work, the various awards were settled by 2 p.m. Mr. Gilbey took the guests and more important officials to luncheon at Cambridge House, his residence overlooking the Park, while the five thousand, or twenty thousand, ate and drank as they could, or just generally milled around.

At 3 p.m. precisely, the Baroness was back to present the awards, amid many hearty cheers for each, to James Nobbs, Wm. Freake, Robert Conk, Ananias Connolly, Jock Lock, Joe Banjory, Levi Betts, Geo. Thistle, Elias Beney, Joseph Balaam and 181 other prize-takers. Burdett-Coutts made a speech, in which he observed that the Commissioner of Police would not allow the Parade to take its planned route to Trafalgar Square "in case it might provoke a demonstration of a more objectionable kind". So, after the final cheers had died down, the drivers were sent out through Gloucester Gate, along Albany Street and Park Crescent to Portland Place and thence via Regent Street, Oxford Street, Tottenham Court Road and Euston Road to King's Cross. After this $3\frac{1}{2}$ mile procession, all were free to make their own way home to stables. Unfortunately Lady Burdett-Coutts and Mr. Gilbey, having already donated once, were forced to find a further £13 each to balance the books because a financial appeal to charitable persons, and especially to the employers of cart horses, was only partially successful. (In modern terms the deficit was therefore equivalent to about £770.)

The *Times* was then in the habit of topping its contents-column with a list, in discreet small capitals, of the chief items of intelligence. The following day, these four were LORD LANSDOWNE IN CANADA: THE TRANSVAAL AND ITS GOLD FIELDS: THE CART HORSE PARADE: PROJECTED SEARCH FOR MR. H. M. STANLEY BY AN EXPLORER. The editor appreciated not only the importance of cart horses in the economy of the capital but also the social position of those who were trying to improve and help them.

This was the year when the Local Government Act was passed. London, with Cornwall and Cardigan and Cumberland and all the others, was now to have

E.B.S Montefiore. 89.

an elected County Council. However, the survival of the Vestries and a large number of Metropolitan Boards, such as that which controlled the Asylums, ensured that the L.C.C. would have less authority than any of the other new County Councils.

In the spring of 1889, Herbert Rymill called a meeting of horse-owners at his Barbican Repository to discuss the slippery streets problem. Stone setts and wood blocks were dangerous enough, but the new asphalt was a menace, and fallen horses were an everyday sight for all Londoners. So they formed a

Spratt's Patent Limited of Bermondsey paraded from the start. This unicorn team won a "red" at the wet 1889 event and was awarded 3rd prize of £2 by the Shire Horse Society.

Horse Accident Prevention Society (Unsafe Pavements), enlisted the support of two M.P.s (Mr. Burdett-Coutts, of course, as President and J. B. Maple the well-known furnisher and Member for Dulwich) and of Walter Gilbey, who suggested that a better name would be the Society for Promoting the Safety of Horses.

The Parade committee was now strengthened by the addition of Mr. Hamond, retiring President of the Shire Horse Society, and of Lord Hothfield, shortly due for that honour, who was one of the judges toiling in a continuous downpour that caused numbers to drop by fifty. The holiday crowd, though smaller than usual, remained cheerful throughout.

The late Miss Isabel Constable had left the Society a legacy (as she had also to the Metropolitan Drinking Fountain and Cattle Trough Association) and the income was to be spent on prizes for drivers who had been employed longest by the same firm, provided that "their masters testified to their good conduct and behaviour and their attachment to, and kind treatment of, the animals under their charge". The first winner of the £2 first prize was Thomas Lansley, who had served forty-three years with Messrs. Smither and Son.

Winners of red Parade rosettes now received from ten shillings to £1 and the gratuity to other drivers ranged from half-a-crown to five shillings. Those who had won an R.S.P.C.A. diploma on a previous occasion were given a horse brass if they qualified again. Jumbo, of the St. Marylebone Vestry (driver, Robert Raynard), achieved the distinction of taking first prize in the Shire Society awards for the third consecutive year. Thanks to the Corporation of London, which topped the list of sponsors with 25 guineas, Mr. Gilbey and the Baroness did not have to make a second contribution this time.

All the newspapers took the Parade very seriously. The *Daily Telegraph* condescendingly remarked that "odd as it may seem to the uninitiated, a cart horse may be a pet to its driver". The *Daily News* praised the honorary director, Mr. Colam. The *Illustrated Sporting and Dramatic News* noted Mr. Pym's "kind heart to all

30

poor working horses". The *Livestock Journal* applauded the wives of the drivers. All paid tribute to Walter Gilbey. The *Breeders' Gazette* (of Chicago) thought that large cities in the States ought to have parades.

Mr. Pym now had John Sloughgrove, secretary of the Shire Horse Society, as his assistant treasurer. Secretary Mole having gone to America, Thomas Dykes, formerly and briefly first secretary of the Clydesdale Horse Society, took over temporarily, and after the Parade Frank Euren was appointed. He was clerk to Sloughgrove in the Shire Society and also secretary of the Hackney Horse Society, founded in 1883. Himself a considerable high-stepper who always took stairs two at a time, up or down, he was to bring his energy and efficiency to the arrangements for many a long year. The Parade offices were transferred to 11 Chandos Street, where the breed societies had their home.

3 Royal Progress 1890–1896

In 1890, the examinations were still more severe. Thomas Chesterman of Leman Street, E, veterinary inspector for the first of many times, rejected eighteen horses, all singles, for lameness, grease (an obnoxious condition to which the hairy-legged type of heavy horse is prone) or dirt. He also dismissed others as having insufficient weight or bone for heavy haulage. The judges kept a special watch for bit-sores or signs of former bit-sores, for traces of injury to manes and tails in combing, and for evidence that arsenic had been administered to make the coats glossy.

Nevertheless, Frank Euren noted with satisfaction in his report that fewer horses were found with ill-fitting or ill-kept harness, and the condition of collars was generally good. (The use of new harness was now very wisely banned.) Nor were there so many instances of chains and other metal work "smeared over with black composition, to conceal the effect of rust and dirt and stable slothfulness. Not a single bearing rein was in evidence." And throat-lashes, "which keep the bridle well set but when tight half-choke animals called upon to exert all their power" were generally satisfactory. Those entries awarded red rosettes totalled 112, including all the teams, sixty-six won blue and only seventy-three of those which had passed the vet received no further honours.

Of course, the horses which needed most help were never brought near Regent's Park on a Whit Monday. But even these were beginning to feel an indirect benefit, because the public was being educated. People might not understand the hundred and one essentials to the comfort and efficiency of a horse pulling a heavy load on unnatural hard surfaces in polluted air, but at least they were alerted to dirt, brutality, neglect and lameness. In the long term this was to be as important for the horse's improved lot as anything else.

Major-General Ravenhill, Director-General of Army Remounts and a staunch committee man from the start, was able to see some of the horses which had been registered for national services under his mobilisation scheme. This was a parsimonious attempt to remedy the United Kingdom's long-established and almost total unpreparedness, as far as cavalry and draught horses were concerned, for war. The French Government spent about £308,000 a year on the breeding of animals suited to its army, and other European countries were not far behind in their arrangements. Only Russia rivalled Britain in her reliance on luck and private enterprise. The British Government allotted £5,000 annually, but until 1877 even this paltry sum had been frivolously squandered as prize money on the racetrack. A Select Committee of the House of Lords was set up in 1873 and, later, a Royal Commission to enquire into the matter. The former held sixteen sittings and the latter toiled hard, issuing its first report in 1888 (and, in due course, its fourteenth in 1911). But neither was of help to the gallant General. Requiring about 2,500 riding and draught horses a year to maintain the establishment of 17,250, he had to buy in the open market and could afford an average of only £40 per animal, a few pounds less than the actual average value. Under his new scheme, anyone who cared to register a horse as eligible for immediate requisition in an emergency would receive a retainer of ten shillings a year. Some impoverished cart horse owners responded, hoping for a fair purchase price in the event of a call-up. Gentlemen possessing potential cavalry horses mostly disdained the bait. Dammit, they wouldn't mortgage their horse to the Government for ten bob – though, if the British did have to fight a war, they would cheerfully *give* a horse to serve for Queen and Country.

It was the General who proposed a vote of thanks to the Baroness for making the presentations. She was one, he said, who believed that "people who were kind to the dumb were always to be found living happy and comfortable with each other at their own firesides". All those within earshot of his manly voice gave her a hearty three-times-three.

Continuous rain poured down on the 1891 Parade, at which the Shire Horse Society's special prizes for singles were won by the City of London and St. Mary Battersea, St. Marylebone and Kensington Vestries and for pairs by three distilleries (Millbank, Thames Bank and Octavius H. Smith) and the Cannon Brewery, Clerkenwell. Brilliant sunshine favoured 1892. The Shire awards, now in the form of equal premiums, were increased to thirty-one in recognition of the greater number of well-bred horses now to be seen on the streets. Indeed, there were geldings hauling coal or refuse whose very brothers were famous stallions that had won at the prestigious Shire Horse Show in the Agricultural Hall and changed hands for a thousand or even two thousand guineas.

In 1893, the police were represented by 159 constables, eighteen sergeants, six inspectors and Superintendent Beard. There were also over a

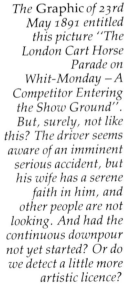

The Graphic of 23rd May 1891 entitled this picture "The London Cart Horse Parade on Whit-Monday – A Competitor Entering the Show Ground". But, surely, not like this? The driver seems aware of an imminent serious accident, but his wife has a serene faith in him, and other people are not looking. And had the continuous downpour not yet started? Or do we detect a little more artistic licence?

hundred officials of the R.S.P.C.A. This was because the Prince and Princess of Wales were due to turn up in the morning, and of course they did turn up. Their son, the Duke of York, his fiancee Princess May and her parents the Duke and Duchess of Teck came in the afternoon. The Maharajah of Bhownugger also arrived, but was late, and the *Weekly Sun*, which rhapsodised over "the young couple by whose approaching marriage London society is so agreeably fluttered", was unnecessarily rude about his shabby brown trousers. However, its other sentiments were admirable, especially in describing the crowded vehicles. "On and on they pass, women and men, old and young – some in awestruck silence, others in the loud merriment of the holiday." The proud drivers received their awards from royal hands – "the heirs of the great Imperial Throne extending to them their little prizes. Thus were the wide extremes of London life brought for the moment into pleasant and even tender association." The "commingling of the poorest and the most exalted" was truly the symbol of "a nation of

free men governed by a democratic monarchy". This Parade was so special as to glow for ever after in the memory. There were little nippers on the carts and drays that would live to boast of how they were there when Dad or Grandad took his prize from King George V himself. ("He wasn't King then, you know. He was only Duke of York and his father was Prince of Wales.")

Here, now, we find the reason for the collapse of the Bristol Parade. No vehicles, no family outing. What sort of bloody Bank Holiday, men wanted to know, was that? One year yet another big Parade warmed the hearts of the Lord Mayor, the High Sheriff, the Master of the Merchant Venturers and Colonel Savile: the next, nothing at all: just rebellion.

The London people, meanwhile, had become increasingly concerned about the continued employment by some small proprietors of light horses, including broken-down thoroughbreds and hackneys, in heavy carts. They therefore resolved that the second object of the Society was "to encourage the use of more powerful horses" for this sort of work.

The 1894 Parade, with the Prince of Wales and the Duke of Cambridge now joint patrons and Walter Gilbey a baronet, was another great success, and in the November the Society moved, along with the Shire, Hackney, Hunters Improvement, Shorthorn and Sussex societies, the Smithfield Club and the British Dairy Farmers, into elegant and commodious premises at 12 Hanover Square, where they found a little space for the British Beekeepers as well.

In 1895, there were 730 horses, 579 vehicles and the Shahzada Nasrullah Khan, who watched the judging with great concentration throughout. He saw 188 red rosettes presented, 221 blue – and eighty-five white, an innovation this year. A further eighty-five entries received no recognition, though only four or five were actually rejected.

This was an important year for the cart horse trade in London, because Richard Tilling opened his new repository at the Elephant and Castle. If Aldridge's in St. Martin's Lane, founded as Beevor's in 1753, was the

OPPOSITE
This is 1892, and the Graphic appears to have got it right. It really was a beautiful day, and the only problem came from over-excited spectators causing congestion round the corner to the left, out of the picture. Our complaint is simply that the artist has given us a generalised coal merchant's entry rather than a particular one

37

oldest mart in London and the Barbican, nearly as old, was the best for heavy horses, the Elephant and Castle was to become – so it was claimed, and none denied it except in Chicago – the biggest in the world.

Only fools and clever men bought at these auctions. Sensible in-betweens went to an established dealer.

The Duchess of Roxburghe presented the awards in 1896. The Duke of Westminster and the Japanese Ambassador and Madame Kato were also there. It was now at last recognised that Vestries and other public bodies could afford better horses than most private companies and could pay more attention to their grooming because they did not work them so hard. So, to the general satisfaction, they were placed in a separate category. The Locomotives on Highways Act, which later in the year abolished the requirement that horseless carriages should be preceded by a man with a red flag, did not appear significant for commercial

Princess May made the presentations in 1893. The driver has his hat under his right arm and one of his passengers foolishly doffs an imaginary one. Two other chaps are making a splendidly extravagant display of good manners and patriotism

38

Dorothy Hardy, the
Illustrated Sporting
and Dramatic *artist,*
depicts a typical, but
un-named, Vestry
pair harnessed tandem

transport because few people used steam power in London haulage and it was absurd to imagine that the new-fangled petrol engine would be able to pull a heavy cart or waggon.

4 Horses' Hey-Day 1897–1903

In Diamond Jubilee year, the rain came down in buckets on Whit Sunday. "Never mind", people were saying. "That'll surely leave the heavens clear and blue for the Great Day in a fortnight's time." Next morning, 781 horses paraded and, though few were rejected at the veterinary stage, 114 were refused a rosette, most of them on the grounds that they were not true heavy draught horses at all, but trotting vanners. Why so many forlorn hopes should have made a simultaneous appearance is now a mystery. Cockerell's Coal Company set up a record by parading forty-one singles. The brewers, too, were better supporters than they had been and the names of Whitbread and Young and Company were now appearing. In the afternoon the sun came out and the Duchess of Montrose presented the rosettes.

The Suffolk Horse Society was now supporting the Parade and awarded eight premiums for horses of its own breed – but only to candidates which had been notified beforehand. The Shire judges, who looked at every animal and had been happy hitherto to thrust a premium at an outstanding one of any breed, now wore a blinker on the eye that looked towards East Anglia.

Supporters of the Shire had always contended that Suffolks were of no use at all in town because their feet were so bad and brittle. There had formerly been truth in this, and "no foot, no horse". But, like the Shires, Suffolks were improving fast as a result of the pedigree movement, and the best answer to the calumny was the increasing number now to be seen on the London streets. Their lack of hair on the legs appealed to some but in general the Shire was still, and always remained, the real urban labourer, even if the Suffolk was a better farm-worker.

The Duchess of Portland, whose husband was Master of the Horse, had the marathon ordeal in 1898 of handing out 653 prizes. "Never", the Committee reported, "has the distribution been made in so graceful a manner." Lady Evelyn Ewart went one better in 1899, with 654. In steady rain she did it so nicely that "what might have been a tedious task developed into an animated display". In 1900 Lady Newton "was actively engaged in the performance of her voluntary and fatiguing duties for a space of nearly three hours". Her score, assisted by a cool breeze and blue skies, was 689, out of a total entry of 777 drivers and vehicles. The horses numbered 918 but a few which had paraded before, and might have been here again, were now far from their familiar London stables. Victims of General Ravenhill's mobilisation scheme (incidentally he had now been dead these seven years), they were pulling heavy waggons in South Africa in the advance against Pretoria. It was the very next day after the Parade that Lord Roberts entered the Boer capital.

Lady Newton presents a prize to an invisible driver in 1900. Her arm-stretching record (689 times) was to last only five years. How many people were equivalent to a load of lime or cement?

Numbers were getting out of hand. It was resolved to limit the entries of any one firm or depot to twenty-five and to encourage four-horse teams, which people loved to see, by increasing the prizes for them. No Parade had ever mustered more than five, because singles provided a day out for more families and friends, and prizes for more drivers from the same firm. The new rules succeeded in reducing the total entry in 1901 by 104 to 673, but only two teams of four appeared, though unicorn teams remained about the same as usual at twenty-six. Ten horses were rejected as lame, nine were too light, one untidy and one dirty.

Yet why, in 1901, dwell on such trivia? 1901! The whole atmosphere of life, and London life in particular, now seemed different. England could surely never remain what for so long it had been. The Queen had been dead exactly eighteen weeks. The shock had passed, and the excitement of at last having Teddy as King (poor man, he had waited so long) filled the spring air. Life was really rather fun, though it was sad that his illness prevented the Coronation from taking place. Sir Walter, Baroness Burdett-Coutts and all the committee were much gratified that he had already confirmed his intention to remain their Patron.

Hoorah for Sixty Glorious Years and a sunny afternoon, with a bit of breeze to flutter the flags! The single belongs to Thomas Moy (1831–1910) of Colchester, who originally traded in waterborne coal but now had depots in London and all over the G.E.R. network. The unicorn team is unidentifiable. (Inset) Sir Walter Gilbey

43

This year of the old Queen's death was almost certainly that in which the horse population of Britain reached its highest point. There is absolutely no way of proving this, because it was not in the British tradition to count numbers of horses, even though they and men and steam were the only effective source of industrial and warlike energy. There were 32,526,075 people in England and Wales this year. Between them, they owned 2,055,104 pigs, 5,534,613 cattle and 18,975,791 sheep. Horses working on farms were 1,316,538, but that was less than half the story. Adding in Scotland, Professor F. M. L. Thompson of London University has concluded that altogether there were about 3,277,000: but he left out pit-horses of which about 70,000 worked underground, and perhaps some others. The present writer also, and independently, has made a similar calculation and believes that there were possibly a few more. Both agree that 1901 represents the apogee. As no one else has ventured to bend his brain so assiduously to this task, the reader may as well accept the Professor's figure as a slight underestimate.

For Londoners, the new century had brought something else new. The larger Vestries had been pressing in recent years for a higher status and authority, and the London Government Act of 1899 had now given it to them. They had been consolidated into twenty-eight Metropolitan Boroughs and one of these, by Royal Charter, had already been promoted still higher and had become the City of Westminster. Any reasonable government might have made this change thirteen years before, but government was never reasonable about London and already regretted the power it had given to the County Council. Now of course there was another series of rows – about whether the new boroughs had too much authority and the L.C.C. too little, or vice versa. However this may have been, it was to horses which now worked for Bethnal Green, Paddington, Lambeth, Shoreditch and St. Marylebone Borough Councils and Westminster City Council that rosettes and Shire premiums were awarded this year.

The parade movement had been spreading recently throughout the country, and the Shire Horse Society now offered prizes or medals to some of the new societies, in addition to London and Liverpool – Oldham, Bolton, St. Helens, Burnley and Rochdale; Cardiff and Swansea; Malton, Brighton, Darlington, Exeter, Crewe, Worthing, Northampton – and Lewisham, which with independent spirit had its own Parade. Some others had begun and fizzled only briefly, but many more were preparing to start up. All took place either on May Day *à la* Liverpool or, London-fashion, on Whit Monday. Parades were also sprouting in major cities all over the Continent.

The Parade of 1902 was billed as the "Coronation Parade". John Colam, Honorary Director, conducted everything in his usual efficient way, and 231 police officers and seventy or more stewards ensured that order was kept. Judging in intermittent cold rain was finished by 1.30 p.m., but the sun broke through while the distinguished guests were being refreshed by Sir Walter's customary lavish luncheon and the crowd was listening to the band of the 3rd (Volunteer) Battalion, Royal Fusiliers.

Attempting to describe the scene as the Lady Mayoress presented the awards, the *Daily Telegraph* reported that every vehicle "was a picture of domestic happiness. Babies had been brought from Bermondsey and Shoreditch, sweethearts from Paddington and Islington, cousins and grandchildren and friends from every quarter of the great metropolis. Here you would see a huge dust-cart lumbering along, its great sides opening to disclose a baby's smiling face and its little brother's tousled hair as he took off his cap and cheered heartily for the prize his father had just won. On the other side, an enormous van with a vast canvas hood came up with a volcanic rumble from its inward parts that was only explained when you saw the lusty representatives of at least three generations packed tightly underneath the awning, and all expressing their fervent gratification at the beauty of the scene. Next to it a great brewer's dray clattered into sight with a bacchanalian rout of girls and boys astride the big barrels, and cheering so vociferously that the huge beasts who dragged them became ponderously excited, and, like the heroine of the immortal poem, started hooraying with their legs.

"One man, in the excess of his enthusiasm at his driver's prowess, fell, with the whirl of a catherine wheel, splash on to the gravel in front of Lady Dimsdale, but was picked up still cheering feebly and replaced amongst his agitated relatives before the cart went on again. In the next waggon, a musical gentleman with a concertina played excruciating melodies of triumph as he drove past the grandstand. In another, a soldier from the front stood at attention while his uncle handled the ribbons."

Thomas Wilson, who won a special coronation prize of £5 for fifty years in the employment of Wooldridge, Hill and Company, the Tottenham brewery, "stood up and said he was perfectly willing to serve another fifty – and he actually looked as if he might, as he passed with a bow and a broad grin into the recesses of private life again".

The Borough Councils were well represented but "parish" and "vestry" were deeply embedded even in an up-to-date journalist's mind. "It was strange that the one parish with an artistic reputation to keep up was the only one which could send nothing to this riotous show of colour and beauty, for Chelsea vestry has gone in for motor cars. However, its absence did not mar the general hilarity." (The change had begun in the last year of Vestry administration, when T. W. E. Higgens, the Surveyor, had purchased two vehicles from the Lancashire Steam Motor Company of Leyland and one from the Thornycroft Steam Wagon Company. In his final report, he boasted that these were the first owned by any London local authority and permitted himself a heavy joke in forecasting that motor locomotion was about "to establish itself upon a firm footing, if that may be said of a form of traffic which dispenses with horses' hoofs". Chelsea Vestry had earlier been a pioneer in the use of steam road rollers.)

The *Telegraph* ended on a high note. The Parade

movement "has not only raised the standard of heavy draught horses throughout London, but by encouraging drivers to bring their families with them it has spread the valuable lesson of that love for horses in which England stands second to no country in the world. To get a good horse first, and then to groom him and care for him well, and keep his harness spick and span – these are the duties which by Sir Walter Gilbey's initiative have now become the pleasure that brings its annual reward. While we remain a commercial country, such work will be of the highest national importance."

It was easier now "to get a good horse first" than it had been twenty years before. The Shire Horse Society's policy of encouraging the use only of sound and well-formed stallions was bearing rich and manifold fruit, particularly in those parts of England where there had been few good breeding animals before. Its annual London Show included veterinary tests in which Professors Axe and Pritchard and their assistants were far more ruthless than when they examined the London workers. This year, 1902, 860 prize-seekers had been packed into the Royal Agricultural Hall for four days and nights, and 476 of them were stallions, many of which were to cover a thousand mares before reaching the age of thirteen.

The following year's Parade, so far from being an anti-climax, saw numbers creeping up again. There were 690 vehicles and 818 horses, of which twenty-nine were rejected. Sixteen were too light, two too small. Four were dirty, three lame, two were roarers and one had a sore shoulder. It was a beautiful day and Jabez Mudge, who had worked fifty-seven years for Richard Wheen and Sons Limited of the Soapery in Deptford Creek, won the Isabel Constable prize.

5 The New Parade
1904–1914

A separate Parade for lighter trotting horses, typically used in retail delivery, was put in motion by a Scotsman who was born in Canada and reared in Glasgow. As a frail young man he sold whisky in London until, in 1880, a friend helped him set up on his own. Now fifty-five, this James Buchanan was immensely wealthy and his distillery vans drawn by Yorkshire Coach-horses were among the most immaculate turnouts in the capital.

He was too delicate in health to be the Gilbey of van horses, and the active role was therefore played by Alfred Dyke Acland, seventh and youngest son of Sir Henry Dyke Acland. Sir Henry, 1st Baronet, Regius Professor of Medicine at Oxford and celebrated pioneer of scientific studies there, was himself the fourth son of Sir Thomas Dyke Acland, 10th Baronet, famous in politics for his independent mind and, among many good works, for inventing what are now known as O and A Level examinations. The Aclands, first appearing on the scene of history in 1155, were one of the most notable families in Devon, and the most attractive. (If this book is dull, it is partly because all the characters are nice.)

Alfred had been a railway engineer, helping to complete the Circle and Metropolitan lines from Mansion House to Aldgate and to Whitechapel. But in 1885, when twenty-seven, he married a daughter of "Old Morality", William Henry Smith – an example which his eldest brother, later the 2nd baronet and admiral, was to follow two years later. Alfred was now a partner in the firm, controlling the stables. Not many had smarter horses than W. H. Smith and Son, though James Buchanan and Company did.

The first Van Horse Parade, on Easter Monday 1904, was a modest affair which was all over by noon because there were only 132 entries. Disappointed spectators desiring further entertainment could have gone into the Zoo, where keepers were performing the ridiculous feat of riding the Grévy's zebras. The Parade's chief veterinary inspector, incidentally, was Professor Pritchard, who thus completed a hat-trick, for he had officiated at the first Shire Horse Show in 1880 as well as at the first Cart Parade.

He was on Parade again in 1905, when he rejected twenty-three of the 182 van entries for insufficient size, lameness, roaring, sore shoulders, dirty vehicle or mange. As in the early Cart Parades, some people had to learn the hard way, while others received their red, blue or white rosettes from Mrs. Acland. Old Pritchard was venerated by everyone, from former pupils to such London carters and vanmen who met him only once and boasted about it ever after. Sadly, this was his last appearance, and he died the following year.

The R.S.P.C.A. supported the new venture and in 1907 gave merit brasses, as at Cart Parades, to drivers who had already received a diploma. The number of entries rose steadily to 496 in 1910, when S. Miller (fifty-four years with the Essex Flour and Grain Company) won the long-service award and the Prince of Wales became President. His Royal Highness' predecessor, the Duke of Richmond and Gordon, had more than once expressed regret at the absence of "the small and struggling tradesman".

Little men, and the owners of plebeian animals, seem to have been frightened off by the Parade's title, which was suggestive of smartly-stepping horses of some size and good breeding. Possibly the misapprehension was fortified by the fact that it was the Coaching Club and the Four-in-Hand Club which donated the long-service awards. Perhaps also a mistake had been made in accepting the offer of three silver cups. The real object was not to discover the best turnouts in London but to set a standard for all. Whatever the reason, Parades were at present dominated by such prestigious firms as Harrods, the Army and Navy Stores, Peter Robinson, Swan and Edgar, Derry and

Toms, John Barker; Pickfords, Globe Express; Allsopp, Whitbread.

However, if the trophies created a false impression, they were soon removed, and not replaced. James Buchanan and Company made the *Daily Telegraph* cup for pair-horsed vehicles their permanent property by winning it at each of the first three Parades. The cup presented by Stewart Freeman of Aldridge's Repository for two-wheeled singles was taken for a third and final time in 1908 by W. H. Smith and Son's Lionel. They showed twelve singles that year (two of them to four-wheeled vehicles) and three pairs – and won fifteen red rosettes. The next day their Mabel muted the celebrations by dropping dead on Ludgate Hill. The Harvey and Company cup for four-wheeled singles was also won outright, by Carter Paterson.

No misunderstanding had ever surrounded the Cart Horse Parade. Cartage contractors' men, coal merchants' carmen, brewers' draymen and City of London or Stepney dustmen were all on equal terms, and knew it, for all alike had heavy draught horses, and some of the best of these did the filthiest work.

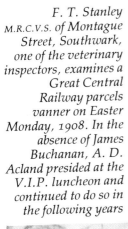

F. T. Stanley M.R.C.V.S. of Montague Street, Southwark, one of the veterinary inspectors, examines a Great Central Railway parcels vanner on Easter Monday, 1908. In the absence of James Buchanan, A. D. Acland presided at the V.I.P. luncheon and continued to do so in the following years

This thought is a reminder that Jabez Mudge from the Soapery was parading again in 1904. He won his red rosette, but the standard required for this was rising ever higher. Grooming and gears had now to be virtually impeccable, which demanded all-year-long attention to health and cleanliness. Special efforts were of course essential as Whit Monday drew near, but could not disguise sloth at other times.

In 1905, numbers were almost unmanageable – 1057 horses and 901 vehicles, 823 prizes handed out with immense fortitude by the Duchess of Newcastle, eighty-one long-service awards. Old Mudge had given up at last, but the Soapery produced another Isabel Constable winner in Pat Regan, with sixty-one years' good behaviour. The Cities of London and Westminster and the Boroughs of Hampstead and Walthamstow each won two of the coveted Shire silver medals, and Bethnal Green, Finsbury, Islington, Paddington and Stepney Councils one. Walthamstow and Finsbury also picked up Suffolk awards. (Like

Still 1908, but seven weeks later. Thomas Brewis, one of four brothers who came from a Northumberland farm in 1870 to start the Tyne Main Coal Company, was a founder-member of the Cart Horse Parade committee and organised the firm's transport until his retirement in 1919. This horse won a Shire Horse Society silver medal

Lewisham, Camberwell nowadays had its own Whit-sun Parade, giving a day of glory to its hundred best Council horses and to the Camborough Athletic Club Band, whose members also worked for the Council, every man-jack of them.) The next year, new rules succeeded in reducing numbers only slightly, to 971 horses and 815 vehicles. One misery suggested that for safety's sake the number of passengers should be limited, but his bleatings were naturally ignored.

In the first week of 1907, 25,000 people filed past the coffin of a very old lady before it was borne from her house in Stratton Street along Piccadilly, Grosvenor Place and Victoria Street, where the crowds stood six deep in melting snow, to Westminster Abbey which was completely filled with the mighty and the humble – who, if you half-closed your eyes, looked all alike in their black attire. Only the costers outside, who saw her off with banners, were in colour. She was buried near the statue of Lord Shaftesbury, her old friend. He has his second memorial in Piccadilly Circus, but hers is just the plain stone in the Abbey floor simply inscribed BARONESS BURDETT-COUTTS 1814–1906.

If Frank Euren had been somewhat preoccupied the following Whit Monday, it would not have been sur-prising. As secretary of the Hackney Society, he had seen shows in Holland, France, Italy and America, and decided that London could do better. Now he was about to prove it. Eighteen days after his Cart Parade, the doors of Olympia opened upon the first Inter-national Horse Show – chairman of Directors, the Earl of Lonsdale; another director soon to become of interest to us, Sir Gilbert Greenall; manager, F. F. Euren. The 500-page catalogue listed in-hand classes for all breeds imaginable, turnout classes for every type of private vehicle, for cabs, for trade (two wheels and four, singles, pairs and teams, with £5 cups galore and even £50 cups), saddle classes, jumping classes. If you wanted to watch in the afternoon, you had to wear a silk hat and morning coat: in the evening, full dress. An eight-seater box for the duration of the show cost anything up to £200. The International was, and remained until 1939, something of which no one

except the elderly can now possibly imagine the atmosphere – the grandest equine event in the calendar.

The Cart Parade was the homeliest – except for the officials. Drawn from every part of England, the judges themselves were the very top men. Some of the amateurs were titled, such as the Earl of Verulam, Sir Oswald Mosley or Lord Hothfield. Thomas Forshaw of Carlton-on-Trent and one or two others among the professionals were world-famous. In 1909, they included Miguel A. Martinez de Hoz, the greatest Shire man in Argentina.

In 1910 the Parade was cancelled. Woolley and Mr. Dillon made centuries for Kent at Lords, but everyone not in white flannels was wearing black or purple – even on Hampstead Heath, where merriment was muffled. The body of Teddy the King was lying in state at the Palace.

The new King renewed his promise to be President of Vanners and also agreed to succeed his father as Patron of London Cart Horses, and so the respective chairmen, A. D. Acland and Sir Walter, were both pleased. By introducing a rule that no more than four vehicles could be entered by any one firm or depot, the

In 1909 Pickfords, as so often, produced the Isabel Constable prize-winner (Daniel Currall, fifty years). But this driver, who has just received his prize from Lady Jellicoe, has a long way to go. The company was equally prominent at the Van Parade. Secretary Frank Euren has a moustache.

53

James Buchanan and Company won ten "reds" at the 1911 Van Parade, but there was nothing unusual about that. In popular opinion, their high-stepping pairs were, with Schweppes' smart turnouts, the élite among vanners. There were 549 entries this year – a number which was to be almost doubled in 1914

Cart men managed to reduce numbers at the "Coronation Parade" in 1911 to a sensible 507, with 644 horses – the lowest number since 1893. Far from hampering the objects of the Society, this restriction promoted them further, for most large companies now adopted the practice of holding a private qualifying competition. Even the idlest drivers hesitated to opt out of that.

It is not easy to appreciate what was involved in gaining a red rosette at this period, when the standard expected of ordinary working turnouts was higher than ever before – or after. Imagine yourself in 1911 a dustman or a carman for a coal merchant or for the Gas Light and Coke Company. Let it be the latter, to celebrate the adoption this very year of the co-partnership system in this enormous undertaking.

You are Carman Grimwood, and just after Easter your Resident Engineer J. N. Reeson selected you and your pair, together with Carmen Harris, H. Banham and W. Banham and their singles, to represent Beckton – the biggest and most famous gasworks in the world on its 627-acre site in the Essex Marshes, just below the Royal Albert Docks. Eight other man, your Co-Partners now, help the four of you give special attention to your harness and horses during the final six weeks' preparation.

After work on the last Saturday, you are minutely inspected, and again next morning. With Linnett and Houghton to assist, you all set off. Even if your horses could fly like crows, it would be ten miles to go. So you stop overnight at the Shoreditch works and do some extra tarting up before bed-time.

Next morning you arrive in the Park at seven, thankful for continued good weather. You all win reds. Drivers from the Company's other works get nine reds and three blues, and three more have supported the Kensington Borough Council Parade, one of the local Whit Monday events springing up like mushrooms. (The Company bought its first petrol lorry in 1907, a Milnes-Daimler, and now to-day has sent six to another Parade, but horsemen can treat this with contempt.)

You get away at last, stop for tea by kind invitation at Mr. Wilson's, the vet in the Commercial Road, and are

Schweppes were equally known for the excellence of their heavy turnouts. The picture is by Fred Babbage, official photographer to the Shire Horse Society from 1899 until his death in 1916. His house in Mornington Crescent was handy to Regent's Park

A real pre-war "shaft-filler". Cockerell's amalgamated with Rickett, Smith and Company in 1899

back just after 8 p.m., when Mr. and Mrs. Reeson run out to welcome and congratulate you. You and the horses are hot and tired, for it has been ruddy sweltering all day. You see to your horses and eventually, the holiday over, totter off home or to the boozer on the way.

A bit different from when you were young, eh? You must have been about thirty in 1889 when Will Thorne started up the Gasworkers' and General Labourers' Union at Beckton. What a hullabaloo! Spread like wildfire, that did, eh? Got the basic twelve-hour day (every bloody day) reduced to eight. Now its Co-Partner Grimwood and a red rosette in Regent's Park. And a silver Shire 'Oss medal.

Grimwood was lucky to get so much help in the stables, especially with the harness. It only happened in some firms. Some blokes had to set their family on the job, evening after evening. Others got the whole street involved. Then, after the Parade, they brought their horse and cart home so that the neighbours could see the rosette.

Pickfords broke an unofficial record this year, when six of their men received long-service awards, having worked for the firm between forty and fifty-one years – as had nine others who picked up prizes in the two preceding years, and others again who represented the firm at Van Parades. Centuries old, the oldest carriers in existence, Pickfords had always been noted as good employers. In the 1850s, for example, they had built a lodging-house in Camden Town for their young unmarrieds, whose behaviour and appearance were thereby refined. Someone from the Society for Improving the Condition of the Labouring Classes had even noticed one of their carters with a piece of music in his hand. Long-serving men meant well-kept horses. Knowing this, the Coaching Club and the Four-in-Hand Club were now providing extra prizes at both Parades.

Before the war-clouds closed in on the sun. Edmonton Co-op, on the left. Cockerell's, at centre, and Rickett, Smith acquired Thomas Moy in 1929. In 1968, the companies were merged with Charrington, Gardner, Locket Limited, now a member of the Coalite group. Charringtons, over 250 years old, have held the Royal Warrant over eight reigns

Moving at last into 1912, we find a sharp lesson being learned by one unfortunate driver on Easter Monday. He would have won the £3 prize for long service, with fifty-one years, if he had not been rejected at the very start for the poor state of his harness. On Whit Monday, the Commercial Motor Vehicle Parade, now in its sixth year, at last forces itself on our reluctant notice, because it cluttered up most of the space between Vauxhall and Lambeth bridges and extended right round the Tate. Of the 270 vehicles, slightly more than half were propelled by petrol and the rest, except for one electric van, relied on steam. There were all sorts of awards – breed prizes for Albions, Aveling and Porters, Fodens, Milnes-Daimlers, Thornycrofts etc., prizes for engines fed on Pratt's Perfection, Shell and so on, and prizes for drivers who had passed exams on how these infernal machines worked. Chelsea Council was in its element and even Westminster, famous for the quality of its horses, paraded a Thornycroft Steam Wagon. The King was Patron of all this.

In 1914, the Vanmen burst through the four-figure barrier with 1,058 vehicles and 1,259 horses – and 119 long-service awards. Even six pairs of simultaneous judges found it hard to cope. The Cart Parade, too, in spite of all efforts to keep numbers within bounds, had crept up again to 732 entries with 916 horses, which gave the Queen's mother, the Duchess of Teck, a heavy task in presenting the rosettes. The sun had come out at noon and Regent's Park was full, as usual, of careless Bank Holiday jollity. The only sign of gloom anywhere was in Trafalgar Square, where all flags were at half mast as a mark of condolence with the Canadian Pacific on the unfortunate sinking of *Empress of Ireland* and the loss of over a thousand lives.

Horses at War

On 3rd August 1914 (lovely weather for a Bank Holiday), the horse establishment of the British Army, 25,000, was pretty well up to strength. Two days later, frantic buying began and it took less than a fortnight to raise numbers to about 165,000. In the November, Sir Walter Gilbey died. He was eighty-three, and it was a good time for an old man to go.

The Army always knew how many horses and mules it had. In the spring of 1917, for example, the total was 868,931, though at what precise minute of what particular hour on what actual day this number was absolutely correct it would be hard to say, because so many were constantly being bought – and so many lost. A quarter of a million of them were already dead or missing, or had been invalided out. The French Army had lost more than half a million. Luckily the supply from the American continent was inexhaustible.

How many civilian horses there were of course no one had any more idea than in 1901. But because they ate a lot and food was getting scarcer and scarcer, and because they were as essential to the war-effort at home as to the armed forces, the government thought it was about time they were counted.

The Census of Horses carried out that April, a week after what in happier times would have been Van Horse Parade day, was therefore an interesting novelty. In London, the Metropolitan Police, who gave out the forms, were too busy to collect them again at the proper time. However, they managed it in the end, and stood no nonsense from awkward customers who resented this unparalleled nosy-parkerism. So there is no reason to suspect that the figure of 101,185 was especially incomplete. The total for Britain was found to be 2,079,122.

In November 1918 another Census was held, but as far as London was concerned it was a fiasco, because the police just had no time to deal with it systematically. This did not matter much, because the war ended eight days later.

A grand total of 529,564 British Army horses and mules had been killed or cast, but there were still 735,409 live ones on the strength. A start was soon made in disposing of most of these and, by 31st March 1920, 560,433 had been sold in various theatres of war and at home, 61,232 of them for meat. None returned to North America, where the British purchasing agents had picked up 703,705 in four and a quarter years.

Pulling Against the Motor 1920–1939

The ravages of death-dealing influenza now at last abated, 1920 opened in a euphoric glow. The Shire Horse Show was back at the Agricultural Hall in February, and the King was cheered ecstatically when he won the championship with his home-bred stallion Field Marshal V.

Entries for the resumed Van Parade were less than a third of the 1914 record, but the crowd seemed as big as ever, and certainly as merry, when Princess Louise handed out the rosettes. It was like old times.

The Chairman was new. Sir Gilbert Greenall – brewer, Hackney expert, pre-war Master of the Belvoir, the best all-round judge of horse-flesh in England, Honorary Director of the Royal Show since 1905 and tireless worker for all livestock societies – had already endeared himself to Van Paraders as a frequent judge. Whereas the late Sir Walter had been called the "Carters' Friend", the genial Sir Gilbert was soon to be known as the "Vanmen's Friend".

The vacancy as President, His Majesty having become Patron, was filled by the Earl of Lonsdale, the demi-god of all right-minded Englishmen, autocratic, charming, "the perfect specimen of the sporting grandee" as the *Dictionary of National Biography* describes him. When they were both in their prime (and they were almost exactly of the same age), he had once floored John L. Sullivan, who figured that, if he had not been an English Earl, he could have been world heavyweight champion. At the International, which he ruled with his iron rod, did he not descend from Olympus in the evenings to dance with pearly queens and hand his nine-inch cigars to their husbands? And had he not on occasions before the war judged London Vanners?

Whit Monday coincided with Empire Day. What a

61

Bank Holiday! Fifteen hours of sunshine. Enormous crowds at Hurst Park, ten thousand allowed free into the state rooms at Windsor, Hampstead Heath back to its noisiest, Middlesex 543 for 4 declared against Sussex at Lords (Mr. Warner 139, Lee 119, Hearne 118 not out, Mr. Haig 131) and, according to old-stagers, the biggest number of people ever seen in Regent's Park. Sir Walter Gilbey, the new chairman of the Cart Horse Parade, was sure about that – and he had never missed since attending the first one with his late father.

And 506 vehicles. Not bad, considering. Considering what, mate? Why, the bloody motor lorries, or course. Mr. Euren, the secretary, reckons the 633 horses are worth pretty nearly £80,000. Inflation, you know. And people needed replacements. Owing to the war, lots of horses had to struggle on long after they should have been pensioned off. Selling like hot cakes at Aldridge's, three hundred a week. Mostly from the Army. In the last two months 44,620 demobbed. After the Parade, you could nip over to Hyde Park – Prince Albert reviewing the Empire Day Parade of all the young people's uniformed organisations, and a choir singing patriotic songs afterwards.

The next year, Van Parade numbers recovered, to 672 horses. One of them was driven by old Messenger, who had worked for Charlie Rickards the Paddington jobmaster since he was eleven. He was now seventy-four, and received a special prize. On a lovely day seven weeks later, 744 heavy horses paraded before Princess Mary, and there would have been a couple of hundred more if the miners had not been on strike. Coal merchants, ever the backbone of the event, were all absent because they had put their idle horses out to grass. Actually, it was lucky there was a Parade at all, because for nearly a month the Park had been a huge Army vehicle depot, in case the strike became general.

Then things shrivelled up. Slump. Farming slump, national slump, the start of the dole. The heavy horse, threatened by the motor-lorry, was protected only by the new hard times which made this smelly thing too dear. Some well-meaning people thought they would like to protect his tail. So they promoted a private Bill to prohibit the practice of docking. Sir Walter, just beginning his year as Shire Society President, mustered a lobby of breed societies and horse-users, and also publicised the reasons why, in the interest of safety, tails were partially removed. The Bill was withdrawn. Road surfaces, though different, were just as bad for horses as in the 1880s, and a Gilbeian deputation went to the Ministry of Transport to meet the Slippery Roads Sub-Committee, but found its members too smooth to pin down.

In 1922, that old darling of the people, Queen Alexandra the Queen Mother, came to see the cart horses and spoke to Blancoe, who had worked fifty-eight years for Pickfords. She could not really understand what he said, for she was very deaf nowadays. But she enjoyed herself, and came back again with the Empress Marie of Russia in 1923, when Princess Marie Louise deserved a medal for presenting the prizes at both Parades.

From time immemorial, congestion and blockages had plagued London streets, but post-war upstarts and smart alecs now began to blame the horses. This was a ruddy nerve, and the popular press enjoyed it.

Selfridge's turnouts, always immaculate, caught the eye at Parades as much as they did in the streets. In spite of the gradual change to petrol and electric vehicles, the company still had fifty vans at the end of the 1920s, and they were not phased out until 1938

As usual, it was the Shire Horse Society which led the defence. It organised all those whose livelihood depended on the commercial horse, and set up the National Horse Association (first chairman, Sir Walter).

To show what horses could do, it also arranged weight-pulling tests at its London Show in February 1924. The King, who was there as usual, saw two horses easily move off with 16·5 tons from a standing start on worn wood blocks. Later in the year, during the great British Empire Exhibition at Wembley, a pair of Shire geldings pulled the equivalent of 50 tons against a dynamometer. But this was not the point. Did horses hold up motors?

The L.C.C. expressed itself in favour of banning them from some streets, and the London and Home Counties Traffic Advisory Committee toyed with the idea. Major W. H. Acland of W. H. Smith and Son (nephew of A. D. and a son of the other Acland-Smith marriage) made a fighting speech at the Van Parade and Sir Walter fired a broadside seven weeks later. Fred Hunt, fifty-two years with E. Wells and Sons, the Rotherhithe cartage contractors, wondered what his world was coming to.

The product of the rumpus, in 1925, was not large – one-way experiments in Long Acre and Mare-street, Hackney. Newspapers said the Van Parade – 738 horses in continuous rain – was bigger and better every year. Actually, sixteen had been poached from Cart horse waters. These were barge horses, permitted of course to leave their vehicles at home. The difference between a Van and a Cart horse, if power and weight is the criterion, may occasionally be dubious: but the one is employed to trot and the other to walk. Did barges really whizz along the canal? (In any case, the Shire Horse Show had this very year introduced a class for "barge horses of Shire type". There were only four entries, all local – from the Regent's Canal and Dock Co., horsed by Thomas Tilling Limited. So it was never included again.)

Princess Beatrice was favoured with brilliant sunshine at the Cart Parade. One rainy day, a colossal jam paralysed all traffic on and near Blackfriars Bridge for two hours. Study of the heated letters to the press showed that this was caused by a) horses and b) motors. The suggestion was bandied about that every London horse should be licensed and that, when it died or was disposed of, the licence should not be renewed.

In 1926, it was the Vanners' turn to enjoy cloudless skies and huge crowds. The Cart men, with a new secretary in Robert Ling, who for twenty years had understudied the good old high-stepper in his assorted horse offices, postponed their Parade to the August Bank Holiday because of the General Strike. Entries dropped by 340, since the miners were still out and coal merchants' horses, as in 1921, were also out, at grass. Medals were offered for the first time to the best horses of Clydesdale type.

In 1927, Sir Gilbert Greenall became Lord Daresbury, and vanmen rejoiced at this honour. He was the idol of them all and when he was walking about in London, as he often did, any driver who spotted him would call out. He invariably stopped to see if the horse was looking well and, after a joke or two, would send the man on his way rejoicing. At the Van Parade that year, Sir George Hastings said unemployed drivers found that the possession of a R.S.P.C.A. merit badge was a great help in the increasingly difficult search for a new job.

The next year, a woman was seen driving a van. Spectators rubbed their eyes, but it was true enough. Still accommodating bargeless horses, the Van people added to their poacher's bag by including Jack, who likewise paraded without a vehicle, for he never had one of his own. He was a trace-horse and W. Harmer, who led him, reckoned he helped others up Wimbledon Hill about four thousand times a year. But not trotting.

In the ever-deepening economic gloom of 1930 when the new "lamp signals" began to sprout from pavements, both Parades, perhaps symbolically, had their largest entries for five years. In 1931 soon after the Highway Code came out and with unemployment

John James Sainsbury (1844–1927), who began work at a grocer's shop in the New Cut, set up in business for himself in 1869. His company's light vans were faultless. Here we see, instead, a bulk-delivery vehicle with a horse which won a silver medal in 1907. The turnout is identical to a later medal winner in 1930. In 1937, the last horses were sold

rising to 2,707,000 (what would it have been if women had generally claimed the right to work?), Sir Walter's usual speech referred to the renewed horse-banning proposals. "Oxford Street," he exclaimed, "is the thin end of the wedge." He and Major-General Sir John Moore (former Director of Army Veterinary Services) stood many a day on street corners counting the number of obstructions caused by buses and the few created by horses.

In subsequent years Sir Walter, always good for a headline, directed his fusillades impartially at the anti-horse lobby and at the atrocity of hatless and sloppily dressed riders in Rotten Row. In 1934, he linked the two. It was the hatless car-driver who was the menace: horse-drivers were a credit to England, and wore hats. He had received two thousand letters on the subject, including one from Japan. The General was now using the top deck of buses from which to reconnoitre traffic blockages.

The following year the driving test was introduced, and there were pedestrian crossings with beacons, barriers on some street corners, traffic islands – and speed limits. The new Minister of Transport, Leslie Hore-Belisha, said he would definitely bar horses from the Regent Street area and opined that it was desirable to get rid of them altogether. This caused a great uproar.

Kind old James Buchanan (since 1922, Lord Woolavington) died in October – failing by a week to complete eighty-six years of delicate health, but maintaining his record of never having done a mean or ungenerous thing. He had won the Derby twice with horses sired by his own St. Leger winner and had given vast sums of money to well-chosen good causes. One may hope the old man had not seen the small wheels with pneumatic tyres that now disfigured some town vans. They were an atrocity, but even a

In 1932, Lord Daresbury (Sir Gilbert Greenall) watches as Sir Maurice Jenks, Lord Mayor of London, presents his prize to Driver Floyd and his daughter. In 1913 W.H.S. had 128 London horses and, though motors were introduced after the First World War, still owned 70. But the stables were closed later in the year and the familiar red single and pair-horse vans were seen no more

purist like Sir Walter forbore to label them so, because they had certain advantages over the traditional large iron-tyred wheel. The United Dairies, always great Van Parade supporters, had this year broken their own record with ninety-nine entries. Each one of them ran on these funny little wheels, like a motor-car's – about as inelegant as a gaitered bishop in brown boots. But even a van had to move with the times.

Neither Parade had ever suffered an untoward incident until Easter Monday 1936, and even then it was nobody's fault. A brown horse, aged six, collapsed as it was approaching the grandstand where Sir Vansittart Bowater, deputising for the Lord Mayor, was handing out the rosettes. It was removed from the shafts but, owing to the crowd and closely-packed vehicles, the ambulance took half an hour to get through and carry it away. The Van Parade, incidentally, was peculiarly addicted to Lord Mayors.

The Cart people were fond of inviting fringe-members of the Royal family, Princess Marie Louise being their favourite. But Mr. Hore-Belisha turned down an invitation to come along, and therefore did not hear Sir Walter speak of horses being able to turn into narrow old doorways in narrow streets, which the motor-lorries could not do. Paradoxically, several London firms were now re-introducing horse haulage, having abandoned or reduced it some while before. Breeding had been steadily declining for years, and there was now a shortage of matured five-year-olds. This was supplied by inferior ones from the Continent, and the Shire Horse Society was calling for an import duty on them.

The next year, the ban came. Under the London Traffic (Slow-Moving Traffic) Regulations, horses were excluded from six major thoroughfares in the Regent Street area between noon and 7 p.m., except for access. Sir Walter said that motor-drivers became nervous wrecks, whereas horsemen remained sane even in these days. This was another homely truth missed by Mr. Hore-Belisha who had again refused an invitation to the Parade. Eleven days later, Mr.

Garner's Bakery of Wembley had five entries in the last pre-Second World War Van Parade. Here are three – waiting for their drivers. And their drivers are waiting because there are 574 other turnouts to be organised. (The waiting-about at the last Parade before the First World War must have been more than twice as long)

Chamberlain became Prime Minister and moved him to the War Office, a most appropriate appointment.

In 1938, Mrs. Lancaster, catalogued as a Brixton salad merchant, arrived on Easter Monday with the oldest animal recorded at a Parade – her chestnut mare Spring Chicken, which at thirty-one was still collecting salads every morning from Covent Garden. Little Jim, owned by John Rogers, an old-iron dealer from Hackney, was twenty-five. John had bought him from some gipsies at Epsom on Derby Day 1920, with his war gratuity. A lady had once stopped him and offered to give him a motor car instead. What a laugh!

Not by their age but in their work, Spring Chicken and Little Jim symbolise the gradual change in the composition of Van Parades. Large and famous firms were selling up their horses not so much because they were unable to compete for speed or economy in delivery work but because they were old-fashioned, which was now a commercial crime, or because of the constant cold war waged upon them. The place of these high-quality true Vanners was being taken at Parades partly by the Spring Chickens and Little Jims and partly by increased entries from those trades for which the horse was so obviously superior to the motor that it would be unthinkable to abandon him. The milk float and the bread van stopped and restarted umpteen times in the same road, and a little horse could do that entirely on his own. Price and Company the bakers were now, right loyally, sending more entries to the Parade than ever before – sixty or seventy; and the United Dairies had adopted the pleasant fancy to line up for the prize-giving in order of colour – skewbalds and piebalds at the head, and then in ever darkening shades to black at the rear.

The senior Parade declined comparatively faster, because a man or a firm either still owned cart horses or he did not. If he gave them up, the gap he left could not be filled by horses of a lesser sort. Lady Moore was giving out the rosettes this year, and Will Ambridge, who had been forty-seven years with Dunbar Wharf Limited, told her he could remember toll-gates on the Isle of Dogs and in Whitechapel, and expressed his

OPPOSITE
Stop! No. 210 restrained at the Van Parade by No. 468. Bernard Murdock, who owns this picture, says the van was No. 7, belonging to the King's Cross Laundry, and the driver was J. Blythe. He should know, because he drove it himself later. The front of the vehicle bears the encouraging legend "Moderate Prices"

71

utmost contempt for the motor-lorry. He also said he had taken a red at every Parade from 1911. This was with various horses, of course, for when one went they allotted him another.

What about John Rogers, though? How would he replace Little Jim? Another war seemed to be coming, but it was a sickly joke to talk about joining up again and getting a second gratuity to buy a new horse afterwards. Anyway, it all blew over, because Mr. Chamberlain flew to Munich at the end of September, and came back with peace. Lord Daresbury died a few weeks later, having never missed a Van Parade or a committee meeting in nineteen years. Every vanman in London grieved.

In 1939, Easter Monday was sunny and warm. So was the next Bank Holiday, when the Cart Parade was at its best – gleaming horses, spick and span carts and drays and trollies and waggons; worries forgotten, concertinas playing; wives and kids riding along, and grannies and uncles and friends too, laughing and calling out to the grinning crowds lining the way.

8 Two Falls and a Recovery 1946–1985

In the second war London horses continued their work by day (who could find motor lorries to replace them?) and endured the frequent terror that came by night. Some were burned or maimed or killed outright, but most survived and none was called up, for the Army could do without them this time. Sir Walter II did not quite outlive the hostilities, for he died four weeks before VE Day. He was eighty-five and, after attending his first Derby in 1875 and the first Cart Horse Parade ever held, had never missed a single one of either.

Parades were resumed in 1946. Though it was believed that, because of petrol restrictions, there were actually more light horses in London than before the war, labour difficulties were largely responsible for an entry of only 179 at the Van Parade. However, all drivers won red rosettes – including the Satwick brothers, both of whom had somehow been completely missed out in the judging. Stewards and marshals, in short supply, had a job to control the mass of cheerful spectators. Seven weeks later, cart horses pulling 197 vehicles were applauded by another large crowd (or perhaps the same one back again) still intoxicated by the great Victory Celebrations two days before and deluding itself that London was returning to normal.

For a time, it seemed to be. The next year, 20,000 people (the police estimated) came and saw 252 Van horses. A pair of these belonged to W. & A. Gilbey, a company which had turned to motors in the first war and now wanted to prove it could turn back again,

In 1946 Frances, Lady Daresbury, leans over to congratulate Bert Matthews and his wife. Pearly King Bert had taken part in every Van Parade since 1922. He always donated a fiver for his programme, and when he died in 1971 he left the Society a tenner.

even in central London. The Cart Parade mustered ten more vehicles than the year before. As always, these were better than vans for Bank Holidays because they could carry so many people, prams, bottles, babies and kitchen chairs. The *Times* commented on one passenger who had "succumbed to the drowsy influence of the day and went through the parade flat on his back, oblivious of the presentation of awards by Mrs. Young." Upon this lady's husband, H. T. L. Young, Chairman of the Ram Brewery, the mantle of Gilbey had fallen. He was also, this year, President of the Shire Horse Society. Reg Brown, secretary of the Van Parade, the National Pony Society, the Coaching Club and, from its beginning in 1922 (in fact, if not in name) the National Horse Association, became first secretary of the new British Horse Society, the product of a mating between the Institute of the Horse with the

74

N.H.A. But this umbrella organisation was not for championing the Cart or Van horse: it was needed to organise and host equestrian events in the forthcoming Olympic Games.

The ban on slow-moving traffic, lifted after the outbreak of war, was re-imposed and extended. New motor lorries and vans were again available, and there was money about to buy them. And so the great horse butchery began. Knackers' yards were filling up. Harrison, Barber and Company Ltd., who had six depots in the London area, announced themselves ALWAYS AT YOUR SERVICE. Smith and Spalding Limited had yards at Walworth, Tottenham, Islington and Willesden, but one telegraphic address found them all: KNACKERDOM LONDON. With thoughtless irony, both took whole-page advertisements in the Van catalogues. There never had been a Cart catalogue, but they paid more for a big meaty horse. Never mind his strength, his soundness, his prime of life, his good breeding, his years of training and his unfailing memory in workaday routine, or his coat that proclaimed the patient hours of daily care given to his health and appearance. Forget his silver medals and his R.S.P.C.A. merit badges. No one wanted him, except Licensed Horse Slaughterers and Manufacturers of the Finest Organic Fertilisers. For them a good 'un and a bad 'un were all the same – plenty of flesh, plenty of bone. At the Elephant and Castle, Alfred Harris was selling second-hand motors because there was only one sort of customer for his second-hand horses. Aldridge's were selling greyhounds as well as cars, and most of the other horse repositories had disappeared in the recent smoke and din.

Illogically, both Parades increased in numbers for a couple of years. The *Times* reporter said 50,000 people were watching the Van Parade in 1948, and 60,000 in 1949. Was he, for some reason, seeing double? He spotted six women drivers, unless it was three sets of identical twins.

In the wind and rain of Easter Monday 1950, dairies (chiefly the Express and United) contributed 93 vehicles and a miscellany of greengrocers 65. They

Part of the United Dairies contingent ready to move off in 1950. No one had ever beaten their record of 99 entries in 1934. And no one ever would.

were supported by bakers (30), laundries (20), butchers and fishmongers, florists, carriers, firewood merchants and rag and iron and other sorts of dealers.

British Railways had just got rid of horses at St. Pancras and some other depots, and so the Cart Parade entries fell to 173, though the new North London Gas Board, the City Corporation and some London boroughs as well as brewers, coal merchants and transport contractors did their best to make a brave show, and the barge horses at last took their rightful place among the heavy Whit Monday walkers. However, being stallions, these elected to respond to the merry May weather. "Untrammelled by barges," the *Times* archly recorded, "one or two were led into tricks reminiscent of the circus, and under their influence some of the usually stolid mares and geldings in drays and carts acted with remarkable abandon." The abandon, perhaps, of the damned. Or were they really celebrating the Docking and Nicking of Horses Act which had settled thirty years of argument by insisting that their successors should wear tails?

Ten years later, in 1960, there were seventy-four entries, mostly small ponies, at Easter, and thirty-nine on Whit Monday. Next year, the Van Parade was opened to donkeys and mules, but none came. "Non-trade and private turnouts" were also invited. Nine turned up and the number of vehicles rose by one to seventy-five, though the number of horses was the lowest ever, at eighty-six.

H. T. L. Young had died in 1957 and it was chiefly the enthusiasm and persuasiveness of his great-nephew and successor John that kept the Cart Parade from collapse: and this was surprising, because people imagined that the only supporters now left to the Shire

Even with a horse from a famous stable, judges bend impartially to their duties. The Shire Horse Society requires feet that are "deep, solid and wide, with thick open walls". Hind quarters should be "wide and full of muscle, well let down towards the thighs"

were old men. By 1965, even his efforts failed to muster more than twenty-four vehicles, of which fourteen were shown by brewers. Young's, not for the first time, entered a team of six driven by Charles Cobbett, who had been with the firm forty years. This was a fine sight and their team of eight, when they showed it, looked even finer. But it was a sign that the Parade was entering the realm of unreality. In the working world they did not need a six (or, for that matter, a four) and, even if they did, it would not be very handy for deliveries. The remaining entries included two old Clydesdale mares. One carted odds and ends for the R.A.S.C. at the Regent's Park Barracks and the other, *sans* vehicle, was produced by the Horses and Ponies Protection Association, which hoped to play a chord or two on spectators' purse-strings. More sensibly and practically Denys Benson, a leading member of the Shire Horse Society, brought the total of animals to 46½ by bringing a mare and foal from East Hanningfield in Essex.

The Van people, who were now beginning to benefit from private driving entries (forty-seven this year), had several times recently suggested a merger. A few men, notably Sanders Watney and Walter Gilbey of the third generation, were active on both committees and this made it easy to arrange a marriage for 1966. A touch of genius produced an apt title – the London Harness Horse Parade Society. Those who advocated holding the first paired event on the old Cart Horse day, when the animals would be in better condition, gave way gracefully to those who pointed out that, if the new society was going to depend largely on private turnouts, Easter Monday would be better because there would be less competition for their appearance from other shows. Reg Brown who, since we last noticed him, had added the Hackney Horse Society to his secretaryships, held the reins.

In the event, there were 172 horses and 137 vehicles – fewer by ten and fourteen respectively than the total attending the separate Parades the year before. Old Joe Fountain was there, as usual. A carman with the coal merchants Rickett, Cockerell and Company, he

OPPOSITE
"Hello! I suppose you're a Private Turnout? I'm with Franklin's, famous from Bedford to London. There used to be a hundred and fifty of us, just on the house coal. But I'm the last, and retire in the autumn" . . .

79

was now nearly seventy and had worked for them fifty-three years. But this was definitely his last red rosette. By the autumn, he had retired and his horse Storm (aged seventeen) was helping with the potato harvest somewhere in Lincolnshire. As Rickett, Smith and Company, his employers had supported the very first Cart Parade ever held. Now they had sold their last horse. And the new Parade, in the year of its birth, seemed on its last legs. The death of two singles having been averted, the pair could soon be buried together. But "the London people" had not done badly. The Liverpool people and the Manchester people, Bolton, Cardiff, Derby and the rest had never even re-started after the war.

As we now know, there never was a funeral. After nearly twenty years, the Parade has more than doubled in size. Private driving is not the sole reason, because commercial turnouts are themselves more numerous than in 1966. The revival is analogous to that of the Shire Horse Society itself, which in 1963 reached its nadir. Since no one wanted heavy horses, they were thinking of throwing the stud books away. Albert Holland, their secretary, went into retirement. He had put in fifty-nine years' service, having joined the staff as office boy in 1904. For exactly half a century he had also been secretary of the Sussex Herd Book Society, and had succeeded Ling in 1957 as Cart Parade secretary. Roy Bird of the Peterborough Agricultural Society was invited to succeed him in the Shire Society and prepare for the obsequies. But he was temperamentally unfitted for this. So was the President of the year, who happened to be John Young. He was the first man ever to be re-elected for a second year in succession – and then remained as Treasurer, to re-model the Society's affairs.

Enthusiasm, energy and efficient organisation multiplied the Shire. In 1921, 7,620 new pedigree animals were entered in the stud book: in 1963, 71: in 1983, 722. In the 1960s, there was a sort of pity for old Fountain. A young driver now is envied because cart horses are trendy.

Of all the breeds associated with Parades, it was of

course only the heavy ones that needed this miracle for revival. Hackneys and Welsh Ponies and Cobs have other occupations than pulling tradesmen's vans. And the true Vanner never was a breed, but only a type. If his numbers are reduced to nil, he can be re-created. But the Shire and the Suffolk, artificially evolved during a thousand years, had come within an ace, in a mere twenty, of becoming the very dodos of the equine species.

The 1970s are too recent yet to excite much historical curiosity, but one landmark worthy of attention was passed in 1972, when Reg Brown was honoured by a dinner to mark his fifty years' service to the Easter Monday Parade. A Freeman of the City of London and O.B.E., he continued in his post, with assistance, until he faded away on Christmas Eve, 1980.

Victorian spectators, could they come back, would find the pattern of modern Parades familiar in an otherwise unfamiliar London. A marvel that would add to their understanding and pleasure is the loud-speaker commentary. From the last years of the Van Parade onwards, Major the Reverend Philip Wright M.B.E., successor in character and individuality to the good men who over the years typified the spirit of Parades, has unfailingly lifted up the hearts of on-lookers, informed their minds and made them smile.

The 1984 Parade attracted 293 entries, comprising 327 horses and a donkey called Ee Yore. Fewer than half were even remotely London horses. One came from Cumbria and one from Cornwall. Almost exactly half were "private", and this was right noble support. Of the 45 Heavy Horse turnouts, one was drawn by a Suffolk, two by Clydesdales, two by Percherons and 31 by Shires, though the Shiredom of some was like the Church of England – claimed by those unable to prove other allegiance. The one Vanner (shown by Carl Boyde, veterinary surgeon, member of the Committee and recent President of the British Percheron Horse Society) had to be Heavy because all the Light were small. The remaining eight seemed to be an over-flow from the Light Commercials, which mustered precisely one hundred. In all classes, some

81

vehicles were orthodox, others non-conformist. But what mattered was that there were so many horses and so many people to see them. The true symbol of prophecy in 1965 was not the old Clydesdale mare begging alms but Mr. Benson's Shire foal.

The following year marked the centenary of the original Society's foundation and there were appropriate celebrations. As on the euphoric occasion when the Parade was resumed after the Second World War, the police estimated that 20,000 people came to watch. No one could question that, because of course Easter Monday provided a free spectacle for all who cared to turn up – this time to see 236 light and 72 heavy turnouts.

At such a landmark, one looks for tradition, and there was plenty even behind the scenes. Who were the Society's bankers? Coutts and Company, still represented on the committee by a director. The treasurer? James Young, son of John Young C.B.E. – himself the nephew of the late H. T. L. Young. Chairman until this year, H. S. Gates M.R.C.V.S., upon whose profession the Parade movement had always heavily depended. And his successor, for a second term of office, the third Walter Gilbey.

Postscript: 1986 and Onward

A sceptic might well suggest that a Parade of horse-drawn vehicles no longer serves any practical purpose and that it thrives only on nostalgia – a delightful tradition like the Changing of the Guard at Buckingham Palace. That would be an error. It now has two functions, not one, and both are positive.

Many of those who take part are impeccable in their standards but there are those every year who are new to the horse-world and are lucky if they have found the right person from whom to learn. They are possibly emboldened to enter by the fact that there is no competition for prizes. At a Show, they would be unlikely to be told why they had been placed at the bottom of the line. Even more discouraging, some Show judges do not give the same detailed attention to the worst exhibits as they do to those obviously worthy of being among the prize-winners.

In contrast, all turnouts at the Parade receive the same attention. After coming under the eye and hand of the veterinary and farriery inspectors, they then meet the judges who check for all other matters – including the vehicle and its appropriate equipment, the suitability for it of the horses, proper and correctly fitted harness and, not quite least, the dress and demeanour of the driver and assistant. If all is approved, a First Class rosette is awarded. If not, there is a Second Class – and advice as to what is wrong. The innovation in recent years of a Third Class is in itself evidence that there is much still to be learned by some. There is still, of course, the possibility of being rejected altogether. Anyone without a First will certainly know why not, but will have enough encouragement to try next year. All this is so different from the atmosphere of a highly competitive Show.

*Lt-Col. Sir John
Miller presenting a
rosette to a smart
trade turnout*

The novice's problem of not knowing where to
receive authentic tuition (there have been in modern
times not a few who set up in this capacity who themselves are not particularly competent) has now been
resolved by the training scheme, open to all, which
owes its existence to the initiative of the Shire Horse
Society in setting up the project 'History with a
Future'. Even before its report was published in 1988,
a training programme had been set in motion which is
now operated by all the organisations involved in driving horses. If all newcomers took the approved
courses and passed the practical tests, already
accepted as a National Vocational Qualification
(NVQ), there might be no problem. Meanwhile, and
perhaps even after that eventuality, there is serious
work for the Parade organisers to do. There are

84

always likely to be people who delude themselves that they know everything already.

The second and comparatively new role of the Parade will be increasingly important as the years pass. Even now, most of those who come to watch are too young to know about the various types of horse and vehicle once needed to carry people or goods about. By listening to the commentaries and watching what he or she sees, anyone can have a painless and cheerful lesson in this literally vital part of our history – a lesson which can be learned almost nowhere else. At an agricultural or breed show, a ring-side spectator normally learns nothing at all and is left with no idea of what to look for. There is no unfathomable and eso-teric mystique at the Parade.

Without an office of its own, the organising com-mittee continued after its centenary to meet twice yearly in the Coaching Club room at the Palace Mews. By 1991, it was clear that it could not indefinitely expect its own members to supply the secretariat gratis as, since the retirement of Reg Brown many years before, was done by John Young and more recently by Michael Simons M.R.C.V.S. who, in addi-tion, was chief steward and was due shortly to complete forty years service to the Parade. An offer by the East of England Agricultural Society to take over the burden was therefore not only welcome but more appropriate than might seem. Since 1963, its chief executive, Roy Bird, had also been secretary of the Shire Horse Society – and until 1940, when that ele-gant property was put out of action by a bomb, 12 Hanover Square had been the headquarters of the Shire, Cart Horse parade, Van Horse Parade and umpteen other societies concerned with horses and livestock. So now Tonie Gibson, Roy Bird's former deputy at Peterborough and now his successor, added the London Harness Horse Parade Society to his many other responsibilities. John Young was made the first formal President of the Parade the next year and James remained treasurer. John Peacock, a member of the Shire Horse Society, became the first heavy-horse exhibitor and actual driver ever to be invited to join the committee.

Money was now increasingly a matter of concern. In 1992, for the first time, costs topped £10,000, more than a fifth of which was for the provision of a temporary stand. Income on Parade day was minimal. Even programmes could not be sold because nothing could be sold in a Royal Park. They were handed out to those who cared to put something in a box. In the early days a driver who was placed in the First Class received an R.S.P.C.A. certificate and half-a-crown for a single-horse turnout, rising to ten shillings for a team of four. Now they had to pay to take part and received a commemorative horse-brass as well as a card and rosette. So that did not help much. The East of England Society's charges were as low as possible, but in spite of generous personal donations and support from breed societies, livery companies and other equine interests, the gap between income and expenditure was widening and the Society's own support for police, ambulance and other charities had to be cut back.

The London Harness Horse Parade was not, and never had been, a society in the normal sense of the term. It was simply a self-perpetuating committee, each of whose members had been invited to join by those who themselves had first been approached in the same way – and so on, back to the first Walter Gilbey, Baroness Burdett-Coutts and the others who in 1885 helped them to get the first Cart Horse Parade going. No one was asked unless keen to offer practical service as well as expertise. Although this informal arrangement was unusual, and possibly unique in lasting so long, it was perhaps the recipe for success. Anyone whose active enthusiasm waned could be quietly dropped.

However, this simple method of procedure had to come to an end, if only to safeguard members from their unlimited financial liability in the event of disaster from any source not covered by the expensive insurance policy for the Parade event. And so, on 3rd

86

November 1994, the London Harness Horse Parade Society was dissolved by its members, who then all immediately signed a deed of transfer by which they became incorporated as a limited company with charitable status. But it is still the London Harness Horse Parade Society and is still run in exactly the same way as before.

Meanwhile, the practical difficulties presented by parading in Regent's Park, so far from decreasing by experience during more than a century, presented a new challenge of one sort or another every year. Whereas in early times all participants were Londoners and arrived on the hoof, many now came from far afield and all in motorised lorries. Parking areas were sometimes changed because what was offered by the authorities one year might not be available the next. It was even necessary to accept the offer by the M.C.C. to use Lord's car park for the heavy turnouts. Every change was likely to affect the easy routing of turnouts to the judges and from them to

John Peacock (Lingwood Shire Promotions) setting off towards the Parade with his team to a 1920 van, originally for delivering bottled beer

the Parade itself. The Park authorities and the police continued to be as helpful as they always had been, but various restrictions continued.

The last straw was the imposition by the Department of National Heritage of a considerable charge for the use of the Park. Limited commercial sponsorship was tried for a couple of years, but it was difficult to secure this without conceding to a company the right to add its name to the Parade's title. The Metropolitan and Royal Parks police forces did not ask payment for services, but the increasing cost of overtime meant that the vehicles had to depart by 1.30 pm. It was clear that a new venue had to be found and members of the committee embarked on a tour of potentially suitable parks.

Salvation came in time for the 1995 Parade – and from the most appropriate quarter imaginable. The Wandsworth Borough Council offered Battersea Park as a new venue – not of course completely new, because the Cart Horses had paraded there 108 and 109 years earlier. There was easy access and parking for the lorries and simpler routes for the Parade. It was more convenient for stewards, veterinary inspectors, judges and all others who had to be on their feet.

Free of charge! Use of the 500-seater grandstand. Tentage provided. The bandstand for VIP guests. Trade stands were permitted and the Society was able to let pitches. Programmes could be actually sold. The Wandsworth Borough Park and Metropolitan Police were happy with the situation and the Council eager to publicise the Parade.

For the spectators, the Parade now became a proper day out on Easter Bank Holiday Monday. No question of turnouts being turned out by 1.30. There was a funfair as well and plenty of catering outlets.

Finally, tradition was not in fact broken. Drivers from Young's Ram Brewery in Wandsworth had won red rosettes in the early days at Battersea and now the President provided horse-drawn transport from the same stables for VIP guests and, as before, hospitality for all the hard-working volunteer officials, while

James Young remained treasurer. The Chairman and driving-force of the Parade movement is still Walter Gilbey of the third generation.

` The first Parade at its "new" venue, in 1995, was also the thirtieth since the Cart and Van Horse Societies had amalgamated. There were 90 heavy, 22 light trade and 140 private turnouts and 9 drawn by mules or donkeys – a total of 261 vehicles and 314 animals. 1996 produced similar numbers, though the trend towards more private entries and fewer cart horses continued and the old-fashioned Van Horse is a creature of the past.

Nevertheless the final sentence of the first edition of this little book is perhaps more apt now than it was in 1985. *Plus ça change, plus c'est la même chose.*

Appendix I

The extant records of both Societies are, to say the least, fragmentary. Where there are no accurate figures, it has seemed sensible to admit it. In some of these cases rounded numbers are available. But they are mostly retrospectively quoted, and have a fishy look. Unless accurately preserved, figures become slightly inflated by the passing of time and then ossify into legend.

For example, the programmes of the last three Cart Parades (there never was one before that) stated that the 1886 Parade had 150 entries, which is incorrect. The first Harness Horse Parade programme (1966) stated that in 1926 there were 874 vehicles at the Van Parade and that all roads near Regent's Park were blocked. The *Times*, which quoted the official numbers given in this appendix, did not notice any blockage, the only unusual thing it saw being a very small pony belonging to a coster.

The numbers of vehicles and horses for the two parades are set out overleaf.

	CART HORSE PARADE		VAN HORSE PARADE	
	VEHICLES	HORSES	VEHICLES	HORSES
1886	102	138		
7	278	383		
8	278	345		
9	222	271		
1890	251	302		
1	333	396		
2	483	596		
3	472[a]	569		
4	539	657		
5	579	730		
6	611	773		
7	645	781		
8	725	897		
9	688	831		
1900	777	918		
1	673[a]	801		
2	680	806		
3	690	818		
4	763	897	132	?
5	901	1057	182	217
6	815[a]	971	239	311
7	721	860	313	373
8	600	717	365	421
9	600	736	457	?
1910	CANCELLED		496	?
1	507[a]	644	549	?
2	561	696	613	746
3	626	772	715	871
4	732	916	1058	1259
1920	506	633	343	?
1	?[b]	744	?	672
2	?	?	698	839
3	839	968	619	745
4	863[c]	986	?	?
5	789	862	631	738
6	449[d]	519	642	766
7	712	801	621	706
8	723	814	?	?

	CART HORSE PARADE		VAN HORSE PARADE	
	VEHICLES	HORSES	VEHICLES	HORSES
1929	739	834	610	693
1930	802	876	651	747
1	694	784	559	634
2	691	?	554	615
3	634	707	613	686
4	605	667	574	650
5	?	?	566	623
6	?	658	527	580
7	?	594	491	536
8	507	574	543	578
9	448	500	?	577
1946	197	231	179	?
7	207	238	233	252
8	217	249	312	333
9	219	250	336	352
1950	173	199	345	363
1	154	176	308	325
2	128	151	289	305
3	117	139	290	304
4	78	97	236	248
5	71	87	210	220
6	64	82	171	184
7	?	60	154	167
8	?	?	99	113
9	?	?	81	93
1960	39	?	74	90
1	?	?	75	86
2	?	?	90	104
3	32	56	85	93
4	26	$50\frac{1}{2}$	117	126
5	24	$46\frac{1}{2}$	125	136

NOTES
a. New rules, intended to restrict entries
b. Coal miners' strike
c. A class for novices attracted 75 entries
d. Owing to General Strike postponed to 2 August, when miners were still on strike.

Appendix II

There have been five Census of horses in Britain, the last of them just over half a century ago. In the second, (1918), London was omitted from the Report because the Returns were ludicrously deficient.

The early Census also included mules and asses. Greater London had 249 mules in 1917, and 499 in 1920, the recruits having come from the Army: but Londoners, like other Englishmen, were not really keen on this useful hybrid. 702 asses were recorded in 1920, but there were really more than that. Owners did not think they had to declare them because the form said it was a Census of Horses.

A. Greater London Type of Horse	1917	1920	1924	1934
1. Heavy draught	28,250			
Heavy draught/Heavy trotting vanners		36,839	27,359	11,915*
2. Light draught/Trotting vanners	42,611			
Light and medium draught/Trotting vanners	—	24,769	23,540	9,596*
Total Heavy draught and vanners	70,861	61,608	50,899	21,511*
3. Under 15 hands: cobs and ponies	16,090	16,857	15,918	13,163
	86,951	78,465	66,817	34,674
4. Used for agriculture	6,408	6,281	5,116	3,683
	93,359	84,746	71,933	38,357
5. Carriage/trap horses	4,718	3,704	2,746	894
6. Riding horses (over 15 hh)	1,353	953	1,323	1,811
7. Thoroughbreds	335	220	435	692
8. Under 3 years, all types	1,420	1,450	817	417
Total horses	101,185	91,073	77,254	42,171
B. England and Wales: total	1,827,804	1,822,364	1,655,627	1,113,579
C. Great Britain: total	2,079,122	2,081,457	1,892,205	1,278,341
D. British Army: total (including mules)	869,931	110,708	–	12,605
Aggregate	2,949,053	2,192,165		1,290,946

NOTES

* In 1934, the 14,834 horses owned by the four major railways and by the London Passenger Transport Board were not credited to counties and towns. The figures given here are adjusted, with fair accuracy, to include them.

1 & 2. The distinction made in 1917 between heavy draught horses and vanners was clear and easily understood. Thereafter, the categories were re-defined in a way that defied the wit of horsemen to interpret. A fair idea of the number of genuine heavy walking horses in these later years can be gained by looking at 1917, when they comprised about 40% of the total. By 1934, they may have been only about 35% – i.e. 7,529, as against 13,982 vanners.

3. Most of these were engaged in retail trade (milk, bread, meat, etc): also costermongers' ponies etc. Between 1917 and 1934, numbers declined by only 18%, whereas the cart horses and vanners had decreased by over 69%. This category was sub-divided in the last three Census – a) animals not exceeding 14 hands, and b) those of 14 to 15 hands. The numbers were 7,819 and 9,038; 6,957 and 8,961; and 6,134 and 7,029 respectively.

4. Opportunities for "agricultural" horses in Greater London were limited. The 1934 figure is about 54% of that for 1917. Nationally, at 548,542, it was still nearly 83% of what it had been in 1917 (662,966).

7. This term caused confusion. Some owners could not get it out of their heads that it might include pure-bred specimens of any breed. They were corrected where possible, but it is pretty certain that cart geldings still lurk here under the pretence of being Thoroughbred race horses.

Further Reading

Only two books are available to those who wish to read more about London's working horses. The first is a contemporary description of the principal types and their owners in the 1890s. The second (to which this history of the Parades may be regarded as an addendum) is primarily a breed history, but also studies the general development, use and decline of the heavy draught horse.

Gordon, W. J., *The Horse-World of London* (190 pp, The Religious Tract Society 1893; reprinted by J. A. Allen and Co. Ltd. 1971).

Chivers, Keith, *The Shire Horse* (xxviii + 834 pp, J. A. Allen and Co. Ltd. 1976, reprinted 1980).